WESTERN INTERACTIONS WITH JAPAN:

EXPANSION, THE ARMED FORCES & READJUSTMENT 1859-1956

EDITED BY
PETER LOWE &
HERMAN MOESHART

Japan Library Ltd
Sandgate, Folkestone, Kent

WESTERN INTERACTIONS WITH JAPAN
EXPANSION, THE ARMED FORCES & READJUSTMENT, 1859-1956

JAPAN LIBRARY LTD
Knoll House, 35 The Crescent
Sandgate, Folkestone, Kent CT20 3EE

First published 1990
© Japan Library Ltd

ISBN 0-904404-84-6

_____

British Library Cataloguing in Publication Data

Western interactions with Japan : expansion, the armed
    forces & readjustment 1859-1956.
    1. Japan. Foreign relations with western world, history
    I. Title II. Moeshart, Herman
    327.5201713

    ISBN 0-904404-84-6

_____

Cover design by Juan Hayward

This book has been set in Plantin Roman 10 on 11 point.
Processing by Visual Typesetting, Harrow.
Printed in Great Britain by BPCC Wheatons Ltd, Exeter

Contents

Acknowledgements

We wish to express our deep appreciation to the University of Durham for hosting the triennial conference of the European Association for Japanese Studies in September 1988: it was a most stimulating and enjoyable occasion. In particular we wish to thank Professor Ian Nish, then President of EAJS, and Mr Louis Allen, Durham representative on the EAJS Council, for their hard work and encouragement.

We are extremely grateful to the Trustees of the Great Britain-Sasakawa Foundation for generously awarding a grant sufficient to facilitate publication of this volume. In addition, we wish to thank Mr Donald Warren-Knott, Administrator of the Foundation, for his advice.

Finally, it is a pleasure for us to emphasise our appreciation of the enthusiasm and efficiency of our publisher, Paul Norbury, which has made our task easier and more congenial than would otherwise have been the case.

PETER LOWE

HERMAN MOESHART

Manchester and Leiden

January 1990

Contributors

ALBERT ALTMAN is a professor in the Department of East Asian Studies, Hebrew University of Jerusalem. His most recent publication is 'Towards a Comparative Study of the Emergence of the Press in Japan and China,' in Ian Nish (ed.), *Contemporary European Writing on Japan* (Paul Norbury Publications, 1988).

JOHN CRUMP is a lecturer in Politics at the University of York. He is co-editor (with Maximilien Rubel) of *Non-Market Socialism in the 19th and 20th Centuries* (Basingstoke, 1987).

OLAVI FÄLT is a senior researcher of the Academy of Finland and teaches in the Department of History, University of Oulu. His most recent publication is 'The Influence of Finnish-Japanese Cooperation during the Russo-Japanese War on Relations between Finland and Japan, 1917-1944 - Akashi Motojiroo, Rakka Ryuusui. Colonel Akashi's Report on His Secret Cooperation with the Russian Revolutionary Parties during the Russo-Japanese War.' Selected chapters translated by Inaba Chiharu and edited by Olavi K. Fält and Antti Kujala. *Studia Historica* 31 (Vammala, 1988).

VALDO FERRETTI is a lecturer jointly in the Faculty of Political Sciences and the Department of Oriental Studies, University of Rome. He has recently published 'Sato Naotake's mission to Rome in 1940,' in Ian Nish (ed.), *Contemporary European Writing on Japan* (Paul Norbury Publications, 1988).

BOB DE GRAAFF is a senior lecturer in the Japanese Studies Department of the Erasmus University of Rotterdam and is editor of the multi-volume series *Documents on Dutch Foreign Policy, 1931-1940*. He is the author of 'Hot Intelligence in the Tropics: Dutch Intelligence Operations in the Netherlands East Indies during the Second World War,' *Journal of Contemporary History* 22 (1987).

GERHARD KREBS is a research associate in the Department of History, Freiburg University. He is the author of *Japans Deutschlandpolitik, 1935-1941* 2 vols. (Hamburg, 1984).

PETER LOWE is a reader in History at the University of Manchester. He is the author of *The Origins of the Korean War* (London, 1986).

HERMAN MOESHART is an assistant curator in the Printroom of the University of Leiden. He has edited *Journaal van Dirk de Graeff van Polsbroek, 1859-1870* (Assen, 1987).

OTABE YUJI teaches modern Japanese history at Rikkyo University, Tokyo Women's University and Ibaraki University, Japan. He is the author of *Tokugawa Yoshichika no jugonen senso* (Tokyo, 1988).

TANAKA TAKAHIKO is a graduate student in the Department of International History, London School of Economics. He has completed a Ph.D. thesis examining Soviet-Japanese relations, 1955-6.

Introduction

PETER LOWE & HERMAN MOESHART

The papers published in this volume were presented originally in the History, Politics and International Relations section of the European Association for Japanese Studies triennial conference, held at the University of Durham in September 1988; they have been revised for publication. The papers as a whole consider different aspects of the interaction between Japan and the West and collectively offer a valuable insight into the growth of Japanese power. The period ranges from 1859 to 1956, a crucial century in Japan's history, extending from the traumas associated with the impact of western imperialism in the first decade of the opening of Japan to the adjustments following the Pacific War, as Japan regained sovereignty after the end of the allied occupation.

Herman Moeshart examines von Siebold's second visit to Japan between 1859 and 1862. This paper portrays von Siebold's genuine fascination with Japan together with the mixture of arrogance and self-interest which was frequently found in the conduct of individual foreigners in Japan. Moeshart brings out von Siebold's cantankerous qualities which often strained the patience of his superiors and the Japanese with whom he dealt. Japanese resentment at the western presence in Japan becomes more explicable when the problems of coping with individuals such as von Siebold are taken into account.

Albert Altman provides an illuminating insight into the functioning of two newspapers in the late nineteenth century. The *Asahi shinbun* and the *Mainichi shinbun* appeared within a relatively short time and the foundations of their subsequent rivalry resulted from the sources of their financial support and diverse political loyalties. Altman demonstrates how newspapers operated and, in particular, how the relationship between proprietors and editors evolved with the proprietors gaining the upper hand in contrast to the previous situation that obtained in Japan.

Comparisons with powerful newspaper magnates elsewhere, such as Lord Northcliffe in Britain and William Randolph Hearst in the United States are evoked in the reader's mind with due acknowledgement to the contrasts. 'What was good for business was now said to be good for Japan,' Altman's concluding sentence, has a familiar ring.

John Crump has produced a thorough assessment of Japanese pure anarchists and of the theory of anarchist-communism as revealed in developments during the 1920s and 1930s. This embraces a revisionist examination of anarchism following the assassination of Osugi Sakae in 1923, the placing in context of the previous history of Japanese anarchism, the growth of trade unions in Japan in the light of the division between pure anarchists and anarcho-syndicalists, the concepts of anarchist-communism as advanced by Peter Kropotkin, and the ideas of the pure anarchist, Hatta Shuzo including the aspects in which Hatta developed Kropotkin's theories. Thus Crump links Marxist and anarchist theories in the West and Japan in an interpretation clarifying the failure of the left in pre-war Japan.

The remaining papers investigate the nature of Japanese government, the armed forces and western policies towards Japan from the early twentieth century to the middle 1950s. Valdo Ferretti focuses upon views within the top policy-making circles of the Japanese navy towards the third Anglo-Japanese Alliance, signed in 1911. Using recent documentation Ferretti argues that apprehension regarding German aims in East Asia and in the Pacific were stronger than formerly believed and that Japan's declaration of war on Germany in August 1914 is more readily comprehensible in terms of the navy's support for continuance of the alliance in 1911.

Olavi Fält discusses the position of the monarchy as a symbol during the Taishō era. Fält is concerned with exploring the image of the emperor projected in the *Japan Times* and the Osaka *Mainichi* and with clarifying the deeper significance involved. The contradiction between loyalty to the mystical concepts inherent in State Shintoism and advocacy of international cooperation during the more liberal era of the 1920s emerges clearly from Fält's analysis: it is hardly surprising that in a period of economic and diplomatic adversity the expansionist arguments implicit in the 'emperor cult' prevailed over the western-inspired liberal arguments of the 1920s.

Bob de Graaff examines the Batavia Conference of 1934 and its significance in relations between the Netherlands and Japan in the years preceding Pearl Harbor. De Graaff argues persuasively that the Batavia talks were more important than previously understood and deserve greater emphasis as the starting-point for accelerating tension in Dutch-Japanese relations. Dutch ineptitude in not planning better for the 1934 conference emerges clearly. The Dutch were complacent and believed they could enforce economic discrimination against Japan. The Dutch colonial empire in South-East Asia was in the same position as the British and French empires: each, to cite de Graaff's appropriate phrase, was enjoying its 'Indian Summer.'

Gerhard Krebs reassesses Admiral Yonai Mitsumasa, Japan's navy minister between 1937 and 1939. Yonai has usually been depicted as a moderate, following the more traditional leadership of the navy in wishing to avert war with the United States and Britain. Krebs pursues Yonai's attitudes towards the Sino-Japanese conflict, the beginning of expansion southwards, and to alliance with the Axis powers. Yonai emerges as militant in seeking to exploit the outbreak of the war in China in 1937-8 as opposed to moderating policy towards Chiang Kai-shek; he demanded conquest of Hainan in 1938-9 and the extension of Japanese control over island groups in the South China Sea; appreciable support for an alliance with Germany existed in the navy and Yonai was preoccupied with preserving unity within the navy according to customary societal conventions. Krebs sees Yonai as leaning more towards militancy than moderation regarding China; however, he fulfilled a central role in the navy, aiming to prevent fundamental rifts from developing.

Otabe Yuji considers Japanese policy during the occupation of Singapore between 1942 and 1945. He underlines the bogus claims of liberation advanced in official propaganda regarding the Greater East Asia Co-Prosperity Sphere. The seizure of Singapore assisted Japanese strategic and economic aims and there was no thought of genuine freedom for Singapore. As in Malaya generally, the Japanese favoured the Malays and treated the Chinese abominably, regarding the latter as those partly responsible for encouraging continued resistance from the Kuomintang regime in Chungking. Otabe sees the paradoxical achievement of Japanese occupation as stimulating the emergence of an independent Singapore a generation later for, as Lee Kuan Yew observed, the young generation experiencing Japanese dominance determined not to be 'kicked around' by any imperial power in future.

Peter Lowe investigates British policy regarding a peace treaty with Japan in 1951. This shows that while the British accepted the American desire for a liberal settlement which would reconcile the Japanese people to an American-inspired foreign policy for an independent Japan, the British originally wanted a war guilt clause, retention of Japanese gold and measures to limit Japanese shipbuilding. The British were less sympathetic to the Japanese than the Americans; they were influenced by memories of pre-war economic competition and by wartime atrocities. The western politician who could claim principal credit for the San Francisco Peace Treaty was John Foster Dulles and he navigated the numerous complexities of the treaty with great skill.

Tanaka Takahiko discusses the attitudes of the Hatoyama group towards foreign policy in the middle 1950s. The then prime minister, Yoshida Shigeru, supported a policy of close identification with American objectives. Hatoyama believed that it was in Japan's interest to cultivate improved relations with the Soviet Union so as to reduce tension in their relationship and contribute to a diminution in world animosity. He was handicapped by the antagonism of Yoshida's faction, lack of enthusiasm of his foreign minister, Shigemitsu, and by his own ill-health following a stroke. Tanaka demonstrates that while there was merit in Hatoyama's aims, the obstacles were too great and it was premature for Japan to risk alienating the United States.

Thus the contents of this volume turn full circle. We commence with Japan being bullied by the West into implementing the unequal treaties as western imperialism consolidated its hold. We conclude as Japan recovered from a catastrophic defeat, including full subjection to foreign occupation, and began to contemplate future policy while concentrating upon economic progress. The articles in this collection reveal the concern for defending cherished Japanese values amidst an era of fantastic change. Japan sought to meet the challenge of the West through relying upon State Shintoism including the symbol of a powerful emperor, and pursuing an expansionist foreign policy in which strident claims to be liberating subjugated peoples within colonial territories were a cloak to conceal Japanese imperialism. The lessons drawn after the Pacific war by Japanese leaders were that a quiescent foreign policy resting upon acceptance of American foreign and defence objectives offered the best means of fulfilling and perhaps surpassing the aims of economic achievement aspired to before embarking on a policy of rapid expansion from 1931.

Von Siebold's Second Visit to Japan, 1859-62

HERMAN J. MOESHART

INTRODUCTION

The purpose of this paper is to look critically at the life of von Siebold following his banishment from Japan and, more particularly, at his second visit to Japan which lasted from 8 August 1859 until 7 May 1862. As will be shown, von Siebold undertook his second visit to Japan after having failed in his attempt to join Matthew Perry's expedition from the United States; he also failed around the same time to join a Russian expedition, driven as he was for the most part by a desire to better his own position both financially and politically.

1830 UNTIL HIS ARRIVAL IN JAPAN

After his return to the Netherlands, banned from Japan because of his breach of confidence, von Siebold continued to occupy himself with Japan and writing his 'Magnum Opus,' *Nippon*. He was often consulted by the Ministry of Colonies in matters regarding Japan. During the period between his return and his second voyage to Japan, the most important result of this consultation was doubtless the letter which he wrote for King William II, to be sent to the Shogun in 1844.

In 1849, in the United States, the pressure on the government to force Japan, if necessary with the use of weapons, to open the country to trade was growing strongly. The cause of this pressure was the concern that American sailors were maltreated if they came ashore in Japan after being shipwrecked, as well as the American plans for shipping lines between California and China for which coaling harbours were needed. The American reproaches about the treatment of sailors were completely unfounded. If one reads the Japanese report submitted to the Dutch Opperhoofd about the trouble the Japanese took while holding American sailors and transferring them to Deshima, it becomes apparent that the treatment some of the sailors received was entirely the result of their own misbehaviour. In the letter we read how some of the Americans repeatedly escaped from the house where they were kept by destroying walls and ceilings, but also how much trouble was taken by the Japanese to keep these men in reasonably good health.[1]

When matters had progressed to the point that the American fleet was being prepared, von Siebold seems to have tried to join it and accompany Perry on his voyage to Japan. Perry, however, was very much opposed to the participation of von Siebold and, for that matter, of any Dutchman. A search was made in the United States for an American of Dutch descent to go to Japan as a translator but on no account was this person to be a Dutch national. In the end, a Mr A.

L. Portman was found who, much later, was to become American consul at Yokohama. Von Siebold was kept well informed of the American venture by someone whom he calls 'my correspondent on board the *Mississippi*.' When in 1852 von Siebold heard about the Russian plans to send an expedition to Japan, he immediately tried to join it. He followed his usual technique of sending his books and articles and volunteering his opinion about the way in which such an expedition should be undertaken. As a result he received an unofficial invitation to go to St Petersburg. As stated in his book, 'With documents confirmed treaty on the efforts made by the Netherlands and Russia to open Japan for trade and navigation of all countries,' the Russians had wished to receive more information from him: 'The memorandum and the letter that you have had the honour to address to me, having been thoroughly examined, has given rise to the desire to receive from your mouth information and additional explanations about a question which no other European understands so thoroughly.'[2]

In St Petersburg von Siebold wrote a letter on behalf of the Russian emperor which reads for the most part like the letter he prepared for King William II. The result of that letter was the same: it brought no change in the Japanese attitude to the outside world. One factor, however, did become clear: the Russian interest in the Pacific area was once more awakened, and the following years saw an expansion of the Russian territory in East Siberia and the Amur region. After his return from Russia, a trip undertaken without the knowledge of the Dutch government, von Siebold wrote his book *Nippon*. In the meantime, the Dutch government, realising that von Siebold might wish to sell his knowledge and expertise elsewhere, tried to inhibit this by consenting to von Siebold's wish to live in Bonn (while keeping his Dutch salary) with the appointment of adviser to the Ministry.

During the following years von Siebold busied himself with the Dutch trade to Japan and made several suggestions to the Dutch government. This did not mean, however, that von Siebold stopped interfering in the Japanese affairs of the Dutch government. For example, he proposed the establishment of a trading company for Japan at Leiden, of which he, von Siebold, wanted to be the director, and he proposed in the same letter to set up an information centre about Japan. The first proposal was rejected by the Minister of Colonies who stated that there was already the Dutch Trading Company which could take care of trade with Japan. The information centre received a more favourable reception, though it had still not been realised. Also in this letter von Siebold asked to be employed again by the Dutch government giving as a reason his desire to continue his literary works about Japan, and to concentrate on the spiritual development of the Japanese people and help to expand Japanese exports. The consequence of this letter was that he was once again employed by the government at a salary of 5,000 florins a year.

In December 1858 the following letter was received by J. H. Donker Curtius, the Opperhoofd at Deshsima:

Translation of a communication in writing from the Governor of
Nagasaki to the Dutch Commissioner. *Siebold*, Dutch doctor.
The interdiction of his return to Japan has been withdrawn as an
act of extraordinary generosity. The above has been announced
from the court at Edo, so it has been transmitted to you.[3]

When von Siebold was informed of the end of his banishment, he
immediately began making plans for his return to Japan. He announced
to the Ministry of Colonies that he wanted to be employed as an assistant
to Donker Curtius and in so doing caused the Dutch government
considerable trouble. The Minister made it clear that he did not want
to employ von Siebold in any official capacity on account of his former
banishment and the fact that he might begin meddling in official
business. To make matters worse, Donker Curtius threatened to resign
if von Siebold were appointed in an official capacity in Japan. Another
of von Siebold's wishes was to bring the ratified treaty of 1858 to Japan.
This, too, was unacceptable to the Minister. After much deliberation
a solution was found in appointing von Siebold assistant to A. J.
Bauduin, the agent of the Dutch Trading Company at Deshima. Von
Siebold was allowed to bring the ratified treaty to Batavia but, as the
Minister wrote to the Governor-General of the East Indies, 'there every
concern of von Siebold with the Treaty had to stop.'[4] Probably because
these arrangements were not to von Siebold's liking, time was lost with
the result that he delayed his departure to Batavia and the treaty was
brought to Japan by someone else. When he finally reached Batavia,
von Siebold once more was lectured on his behaviour in Japan: he had
to refrain from any interference in politics; it was also made quite clear
to him that he went to Japan as a private person, in the employment
of the Dutch Trading Company.

THE SECOND VISIT IN JAPAN

Von Siebold arrived in Nagasaki on 8 August 1859 in the company of
his young son, Alexander, and took lodgings in one of the city's many
Buddhist temples. In a letter from A. J. Bauduin to his sisters in
Holland, we are given a glimpse of the impression the old man must
have made:

> 'Mr von Siebold lives in Nagasaki in a temple. I visit him from
> time to time and like everyone here His Honour is being put to
> hard shifts at his age and for someone who has been accustomed
> to a comfortable life, such is not easy, but I must say that His
> Honour is keeping himself well enough, even if things are not as
> at home.
>   Seldom have I seen a man so over-decorated as papa von Siebold.
> Crosses and grand-crosses of all nations; in his colonel's uniform
> His Honour looks magnificent, quite a contrast with the modest
> Japanese.'[5]

In October of that year von Siebold started one of the strangest
undertakings in his career: he opened a printer's shop at Deshima. The
idea behind this is not quite clear. Apart from a few articles by von

Siebold himself, the printer's shop only printed some business papers for the Dutch traders in Nagasaki. Probably von Siebold's continual thirst for money was the reason for the enterprise. He succeeded, however, in having the printer, G. Indermauer, who had been assistant to the doctor at Deshima, sent out from Batavia, and he obtained substantial credits from the government of the Dutch East Indies.

In the meantime, von Siebold had begun to make contact with the Japanese authorities. Within the first days of his arrival there exists a curious letter to the Governor of Nagasaki in which he offers amongst other items European suits of armour for sale, stating that they are among the best of their kind and that such armour is worn by all the guards in the European courts.[6] Less innocent, and in direct contradiction to his orders, were his talks with the governor in which he advised about matters of a political and military nature. It was quite easy for him to do so because the Japanese believed him to be in Japan in an official capacity. For his part, von Siebold did nothing to clear up this misunderstanding. He kept wearing his colonel's uniform, though no longer in active service, and he impressed both the Japanese and foreigners with his decorations. He also irritated them and some of this annoyance is discernible in one of the letters of Albert Bauduin:

> From time to time I receive a visit from Mr P. F. von Siebold, the author of a large work about Japan, a work which must have involved considerable time but which is so large that nobody reads it. Mr von Siebold is here, as he says, to complete that work, but at the same time he is an adviser to the Dutch Trading Company, which means that I am authorised, if I think it useful, to consult His Honour. His Honour is absolutely not in the service of the Dutch Government and has nothing to say about government money or merchandise. His Honour is simply a private person who came here to finish his work, that is all.
>
> Mr von Siebold is 64 years old and is undoubtedly a very strong man. On Easter Day the inhabitants of Deshima took a walk in the mountains, from 8 o'clock in the morning until 6 o'clock in the evening. His Honour took part in this like a young man of 20 years of age. His Honour brought a son of 13 years, a nice lad, who would like it better to be at home with his mother than with his father in Japan. Well, for a child of his age it is not very attractive to stay with an old scientist in Japan.[7]

Towards the end of 1860 it became clear that the contract with the Dutch Trading Company was not going to be renewed. The company was not satisfied with the way von Siebold had discharged his responsibilities. This was not surprising in view of the fact that von Siebold perceived his adviser's job only as a disguise for his presence in Japan. His real purpose in that country was the completion of his work and the improvement of his own position. When he discovered that the Dutch Trading Company would employ him for no longer, he made known to the Governor of Nagasaki that he was willing to stay in Japan as an adviser to the Japanese government. Soon afterwards, an invitation to stay on followed. Without waiting for the permission of the Dutch government, von Siebold accepted this invitation and asked the Dutch Vice-Consul at Nagasaki, J. P. Metman, to send a letter to the governor stating that the Dutch government did not object. Metman refused to do this, as he wrote in a confidential letter to his superior, Mr J. K. de Wit, the Dutch Consul-General, who was at that time in Edo. Metman wrote that von Siebold had told him that he had given advice about the military strengthening of a bay in the proximity of Nagasaki and that he was busy making a plan for the strengthening of the Bay of Nagasaki. Metman foresaw great trouble with the other foreign powers in Japan if this advice became public because Japan might use these military installations against them.[8]

In March 1861 the Japanese authorities requested permission of the Dutch consulate in Nagasaki to let von Siebold go to Kanagawa. De Wit answered that it was not his concern where von Siebold went, as he was not acting in an official position in Japan. But the Japanese did not understand this and sent the following letter to De Wit:

> Your letter No. 8 of the 23rd Siogoeats or March 4th, 1861, has been read. Because the translation in this letter, that von Siebold is not present in an official capacity, is not clear to us, we have asked the translator and he answered: the meaning of this is so, that your concern is not with the teaching of von Siebold, here or in Kanagawa after his arrival, and he can go as decided, but in case fortune or misfortune may happen to him, Your Honour will be concerned. So we trust that Your Honour's opinion about his visit to Kanagawa is like this, but once more we ask if this is so. With honour and respect, 28th day of the 1st month of the 2nd year of Manen. *Signed Okabe Suruga no Kami.*[9]

Before he left for Kanagawa, von Siebold had several meetings with the governor in which he gave his advice about Nagasaki harbour and the creation of a free port. On 19 April, still in the company of his son, Alexander, von Siebold arrived at Yokohama. There his arrival was awaited with impatience by the Japanese authorities. The Dutch Consul at Nagasaki, Dirk de Graeff van Polsbroek, was already aware of this impatience. On several occasions the Japanese authorities had asked him questions about von Siebold and requested information about the kind of house to be made ready for him. According to his letter of 28 April to De Wit, de Graeff finally ran out of patience:

> After the arrival of Mr von Siebold in this port, the Governor of Kanagawa sent one of his officers to me to enquire if Mr von Siebold wanted to move to his house at once. I told my clerk to answer that they should address such a question to Mr von Siebold himself and not to me.
>
> The next morning the Governor again sent some of his officers with the question as to what kind of bed should be prepared for Mr von Siebold. Fearing that such questions, which had nothing to do with me, would never end, I visited the Governor and asked him never to bother me again with such questions, that I had told his predecessor clearly that Mr von Siebold was not a civil servant of the Dutch Government and that I could not concern myself

with the lodging of private persons.

The Governor, very surprised, replied that he had received the message from Nagasaki to the effect that Mr von Siebold was a civil servant of the Dutch Government which had sent him to Nagasaki. On this I have answered that Mr von Siebold had been dismissed long ago but that he had obtained permission to continue wearing his uniform, that he had come to Nagasaki as an adviser to the Dutch Trading Company and that the Dutch government had helped him with money to establish a printing business.

After this, the Governor asked me how Mr von Siebold should be received. I answered that he should know better than I since the Japanese Government had invited him and I did not know in what position he had come here. The Governor declared that he would hold no position whatever and had come only to clear up an important question and that he was very surprised that von Siebold had not brought furniture or anything with him, because in Japan it was customary to bring one's own furniture if one rented a house. I said that he should say all this to Mr von Siebold directly.

A few days later, speaking with the French Consul-General, I told him what I had said to the Governor but I only succeeded in convincing him after much effort that Mr von Siebold had come to Japan without the request of our Government. The Vice-Consul of the Netherlands, *(signed) D. de Graeff van Polsbroek.*[10]

On 23 April von Siebold had his first interview with the Governor of Kanagawa and he sent a report to the Minister of the Colonies. At this interview a number of Metsuke and translators were present and everything von Siebold said was written down and reported to the Japanese government. Von Siebold's political sympathies - he was very pro-Russian - emerge clearly. The governor asked von Siebold's opinion about the various states that had concluded treaties with Japan. England, according to von Siebold, would go to war to defend their trade routes; of America the same was true though to a lesser extent than for England. From France it was the export of its lively spirit that was to be feared. The comments on Russia are interesting enough to quote here in full:

The Emperor of Russia aimed with the conclusion of a treaty with Japan in the first place at a relationship of peace and trade so as to supply his people living in the cold and barren areas of Northern Asia with food in emergencies and to secure for his fleet safe harbours and food in the waters of Japan and China for the protection of his possessions; when the Emperor, as it has happened, expands his territories in the North of Japan, he is doing so with the aim not to let other countries which could be less peaceful neighbours than Russia conquer these areas. From the side of Russia, Japan never has to fear hostilities if Japan does not invite them.[11]

The above quotation is taken from the report of von Siebold to the Minister of Colonies. Dirk de Graeff van Polsbroek gave another account of this conference in his letter to the consul-general:

To-day I have pumped the translator who was present at the conference which Mr von Siebold had with the Governor of Kanagawa and he has told me that Mr von Siebold had said that of all the nations having treaties with Japan, Prussia and Russia would be the best friends of Japan. After this Mr von Siebold said that if Japan would send Ambassadors to Europe, they should also visit Russia and finally that he was sure that England and France would soon occupy an island lying on the East of Japan to provide a base for their warships, and that if Japan would consent to yield to Russia a part of the territories in the North of Japan, it could be sure that Russia would assist Japan in case trouble might arise between the Japanese Empire and those two nations.

The name of the island has not been mentioned by Mr von Siebold. The translator thought he might be thinking of 'Moening Shima' (See my letter of 21 March, Lett. A. Secret). The conference lasted from 11 o'clock in the morning until 2 o'clock in the afternoon and when he took his leave, the Governor told Mr von Siebold that he would receive him next time in his house at Kobe.

Politely, I ask Your Honour to be very careful with this information, since the translator who told me this certainly would have to pay with his head for his carelessness if this information became known.[12]

The remarks of von Siebold were, of course, reported to the Governor-General of the East Indies and from there to The Hague. Already, for some years, Russian movements in East Asia had been followed with suspicion by the other western nations. Russian expansion in eastern Siberia and the Amur region pointed to the fact that Russia wanted to become a power of some significance in the Far East. When de Graeff had been appointed vice-consul at Kanagawa by Donker Curtius, one of the articles in his instructions had ordered him explicitly to watch the Russians and report every move they made. Just before von Siebold's arrival at Yokohama, Dirk de Graeff had invited an officer of a Russian navy ship to dinner and, after filling him full of wine, had extracted from him the information that at Kronstadt, a Russian naval base, six of the largest warships were lying ready to be dispatched to Japan. Also, in those days there were rumours that Russia wanted to occupy Hokkaido.

It would be interesting to read the Japanese reactions to von Siebold's remarks. To my regret I have not seen these but one cannot imagine that the Japanese authorities would have taken pleasure in von Siebold's counsel. In early May 1861 von Siebold was transferred to Edo where he was lodged in the same buildings where Count Eulenburg, the Prussian ambassador, had been staying. The conferences with the Japanese authorities continued and again von Siebold advised against the policies of the Dutch government and the other western nations: in the case of those nations which tried to obtain the opening of more harbours to trade, von Siebold advised the Japanese to close all of them except Nagasaki. Evidently, such advice, which sooner or later, had to become known to the foreign diplomats, was unlikely to be well received. One of the von Siebold stories, however, turned out to be true. Tsushima was occupied by a western power, not by England or France, but by Russia. Captain Berileff of the Russian fleet put a part of his crew ashore, built houses, a bath, made a road and fought with the Japanese on the island. According to the reports of Commander Craigie of the English warship, *Ringdove*, and Laurence Oliphant who accompanied him on this inspection, Dutch and English diplomatic pressure in St Petersburg finally secured the departure of the Russians from the island in the closing months of that year. Von Siebold, without any knowledge of the diplomatic action being taken, spoke of a misunderstanding and he always believed that the departure of the Russians was caused by a letter which he had written to his personal friend, the Russian admiral, Likhatschoff.[13]

The turning point in von Siebold's stay at Edo, and for that matter in Japan, came with the attack on the British Legation in Edo in July. The night after the return of the English minister, Rutherford Alcock (who had made the journey from Nagasaki to Edo in the company of the Dutch consul-general, de Wit), the British Legation was attacked by a group of *ronin*. Von Siebold was notified about this and early in the morning he went to the legation where, according to his own report, he treated several wounded, though the legation had two medical doctors available. Later he wrote an extensive report entitled, 'The attack on the English Legation in the Tozenji temple at Edo, historically and politically explained by Mr P. F. von Siebold.'[14] Although arriving several hours after the attack, he claimed to be able to judge the incident and, as he wrote, he went to a considerable amount of trouble to calm the excited British minister and his French colleague who had arrived on the scene. Von Siebold's interference appears to have angered Rutherford Alcock who seems to have thrown von Siebold out of his legation.

A short time later de Wit met the above-mentioned diplomats and it is easy to guess what was the subject of this conference. The meddling of von Siebold and his inclination to take up a position between the Japanese government and these ministers was one of the reasons that de Wit asked the Japanese authorities to dismiss von Siebold. The Dutch government had further cause for considering this request, such as the critical comments of other diplomats that the Netherlands had two ambassadors in Japan and the fact that von Siebold accepted a large salary from the Japanese government (400 ryō per month) while continuing to receive a salary from the Dutch government. The position of the official representative of the Netherlands, Consul-General de Wit, was also at stake: the Japanese government consulted von Siebold instead of de Wit or de Graeff van Polsbroek.

In November 1861 von Siebold left Edo and returned to Kanagawa, disappointed but by no means disheartened. He told van Polsbroek, the Dutch consul in Kanagawa, that he would return to Nagasaki but he did not want to leave Japan as he was awaiting appointment as consul-general of the Netherlands in Japan, which he was sure the Dutch king would bestow upon him.[15] From the Japanese government he had secured a declaration of no objection against his return in an official position. In Nagasaki, however, orders to return at once to Batavia were waiting for him.

CONCLUSION

When considering the facts about von Siebold as detailed above, one cannot help wondering about the personality of the man. Regarding his second visit to Japan, I believe that it was characterised by complete self-exaltation. How could he possibly claim to be the only one with sufficient knowledge about Japan while being absent from that country for nearly thirty years - depending as he did on reports from others, who often were not very reliable sources of information. Von Siebold was a very difficult man to live with and, though his contemporaries in Japan rarely wrote about him, when they did so they were sometimes quite critical of him. One of them, arriving shortly after von Siebold in Nagasaki, wrote that von Siebold had managed to pick quarrels with everyone except the Russians. In a letter by von Siebold's brother-in-law, Karl von Gagern, he states: 'Siebold likes to help and serve but, if I may say so, he has a certain egoism in the way he serves, in other words, he wants, when he helps, to help *alone*, especially if it concerns Japanese affairs.'[16]

In Japan the members of the Japanese government who met him probably experienced the same thing. Reading through the reports of his conferences with the Japanese authorities, it is clear that von Siebold had the same attitude in Japan when giving advice or explaining foreign sciences or techniques to them. This probably shows also why de Wit did not need too much pressure on the Japanese government to secure his return to Nagasaki.

Reference was made earlier to the printing business at Deshima. To enable him to open the premises he obtained a credit from the Dutch government in Batavia in the sum of 10,000 florins - to be repaid by him later - but also a salary of 4000 florins. It appears from signed documents in the national archives at The Hague that he received this money within a short period. There are no documents saying what he did with this money which for those days was an enormous amount. His statement to the Japanese authorities that he was without means was untrue. The Dutch government was justly indignant with his statement. As noted above, he received an annual salary of 5000 florins which went for the most part to his wife in Europe. But with the money from the printer's shop it could hardly be said that he was in financial difficulties. More to the point, it seems that von Siebold was very greedy. After his return in Batavia he wrote an extensive document to justify himself in the eyes of the Dutch government,[17] and tried to show that his disappointing experience in Japan was the fault of de Wit whom he more or less accused of jealousy. But he carefully omitted a number of events which might have shed a less favourable light on his own behaviour. He made the mistake of writing in this document that the Japanese government had paid him on his return to Nagasaki, in addition a substantial amount of money as well as the cost of his voyage to

Batavia. Someone in the Ministry wrote next to this sentence the words, 'which he also had paid to him later by the Dutch East Indies.'

Furthermore, his evident greed was obviously connected with the very strange affair of the ship which von Siebold tried to sell to the Japanese government. In the event the deal did not go through but this was not for want of trying by von Siebold. He had busied himself intensely with the embassy which the Japanese government intended sending to Europe. He wanted to go himself as an adviser but to the exclusion of any other European. He, von Siebold, would introduce the Japanese envoys at the courts of Europe. He was quite successful in promoting this idea; then he tried to persuade the Japanese government that it would be in their best interests if the Japanese embassadors travelled in their own ship, in fact he could introduce them to an excellent bargain - the ship *Lycemoon* belonging to Dent & Company. The *Lycemoon* was a relatively new ship which von Siebold proposed to fill with porcelain and laquerware which he would sell at a profit in Europe.[18] The Japanese government decided to let the embassy travel in the British warship, *Odin*, and in doing so made a much wiser choice than they could have realised at the time, because a few weeks later one of the boilers of the *Lycemoon* exploded. What could have prompted von Siebold to make such a proposal to the Japanese authorities other than greed for money? He of all people must have known that the senior officials selected to represent the Japanese empire in Europe would never consent to travel as merchants - at that time considered the lowest social class in Japan.

Following his return from Japan in 1830, von Siebold set about exploiting his special knowledge of Japan for his own profit. After writing *Fauna Japonica*, *Flora Japonica* and *Nippon*, a scientific achievement of the first order, he set out to promote his name and reap whatever rewards he could from it. The technique he used was to send his works and articles to the various monarchs in Europe who, in return, sent him decorations. In one of the reports of the Ministry of Colonies, someone remarked that von Siebold 'collected' decorations.[19] His behaviour in Japan, trying to obtain a position between the Japanese government and the foreign representatives, was the result of von Siebold's urge to better his own position but he also wanted to shield Japan against too great an influence of the foreign nations.[20] The fact that the foreign representatives did not want his interventions simply did not register with him. In the above-mentioned report written in Batavia, he wrote about his excellent relations with the foreign diplomats. These critical observations do not mean that von Siebold should not be honoured as the great scientist he was. It was most unfortunate that in his later years von Siebold concentrated more on politics and money than on science. But as it is, all men, even the greatest, have their faults, though von Siebold would have been the first to deny this statement.

NOTES   ARA indicates National Archives at The Hague in The Netherlands.

1. ARA, Nederlandsche Factorij in Japan, No. 1632. Translation of the events regarding the shipwrecked sailors. The 7th gogats 1848 fifteen American whale-hunters, because of shipwreck, approached the land of Matsmai in boats. The 2nd Rokugats of the same year one man landed on the island Lisili belonging to Yesso.

All of them landed and asked for help, so they were given shelter. Then, John Buwl and Robert Macoy broke through the roof of the toilet and escaped, but they were found in the mountains and were recaptured.

After that John Martin and again Robert Macoy broke through the roof of the room, but they were again caught. Because the three mentioned persons behaved so badly, they were kept in a locked place while being sent here in the ship, but on arrival of the ship, having been questioned, they asked to be forgiven and on that occasion they were told to behave well, then they agreed to behave according to the warning. Because of that they were taken from the locked place and put in the large room with the others and they received care.

Because now the time has come for the Dutch ship to leave this bay, the Opperhoofd has written a letter to them to warn them not to behave badly, and they have answered in writing to listen to this.

On the night of the 27th Kugats Robert Macoy took away the boards of the room and escaped, in the meantime he has been taken, after questioning he has been kept in a place by himself, but his declaration has been accepted, and because of kindness he has been sent back to the other room and the others have been earnestly warned too.

The 18th Zuitsigats John Buwl, Robert Macoy and Jacob Boyle escaped by secretly burning the floor of the room but they were caught in the farmhouse. On that occasion the others were asked, too, but their answer was impolite and unacceptable. As stated above John Buwl and the other two persons were allowed from the locked place in the ship to be free after they asked forgiveness; after that all were warned by the Opperhoofd, but they behaved badly on many occasions, so it was not possible to be sure about the others, but supposing they were to behave more and more badly, they would all be imprisoned. The sick among them have been treated as follows: Moke was hit by heat in the evening of the 6th Hatsigats but he recovered with medicines. Robert Macoy had abdominal pains since the 19th of the same month, but recovered with medicines. Moke, James Hall, Mama and Steam had a cold since the same day, but they recovered with medicines. John Martin had since the same day fever because of toothache, but he recovered with medicines. Manly and Hirim had a cold since the 20th Hatsigats, but recovered with medicines. John Waters had had fever and abdominal aches since the 20th Hatsigats but recovered with medicines. Since the 4th of the same month, Steam had a swelling but he recovered; after that he got moist cough, but again he recovered with medicines.

Regarding the death of Manly, in the night of the 12th Zuitsigats, the others made known that he had hanged himself after they went to sleep; the reason of this has been investigated, but they declared that none of them knew about this, at their request the body has been buried. Jacob Boyle has had stomach ache since the 5th Siogats but he recovered with medicines. John Buwl has had an inflammation of his face since the 8th Siogats but he recoved with medicines. John Waters had a cold since the 15th Siogats, but he recovered with medicines. John Buwl had a swelling but recovered with medicines. Melcher Biffar since the 19th Sangats and James Hall since the 24th had swellings, they are still taking medicines. Harry Barker and Jack are never sick. Ranald Macdonald who came to the island Lisili has never been ill.

From the above the Opperhoofd must make known that they have all been provided with not only clothes but also with other necessities, as required; and in particular that they oppose the laws of this country. Deshima, 2nd Siogats 1849 (24 April).

2. ARA, Koloniën, Geheim Verbaal, No. 5841. Letter of von Siebold dated April 7, 1853.

3. ARA, Nederlandsche Factorij in Japan, No. 1641.

4. ARA, Koloniën No. 793. Letter of Minister of Colonies, Rochussen, to the Governor-General of the Dutch Indies, dated February 25, 1859. Lett. A. No. 6/242. [...]The act of ratification of the Treaty concluded with Japan on the 18th of August last will be given to you by Mr von Siebold, you will please act in the sending of this document to the Dutch Commissioner in Japan as laid down in my secret dispatch of to-day No. 82.F, and the exertions of Mr von Siebold with this matter has to be regarded as ended on his arrival in Batavia.[...]

5. ARA, Aanwinsten 1" Afdeling., 1965, 15.

6. ARA, Koloniën, Geheim Verbaal No. 5923.

23 May 1860. To His Excellency the Governor of Nagasaki.

Your Excellency.

At the occasion of the audience of August 8th, I had the honour to ask your special attention for the Dutch Trading Company which now, under the direction of Mr A. J. Bauduin and my cooperation as adviser, has established an agency in Japan. This large and solid Trading Company under the protection of His Majesty the King of the Netherlands, will continue from now on the ages old trade relations between the Netherlands and Japan and specially provide the Japanese Government with all they might need from the Netherlands or the Dutch Indies.

Goods of all kinds, steamships, steam-engines, weapons and armour, this Company that pays more attention to the development of industry than to gain, will be able to supply at most profitable costs to the Japanese Government and receive in payment produce of the country suitable for export. The Company will accept orders of the largest size and deliver speedily.

I shall take on the liberty to offer to Your Honour a list of weapons and armour which the Company has imported as a proof. The suits of armour selected by me at request of the Company, I declare very suitable for the high officers and the bodyguard of His Majesty the Emperor, as the bodyguards of most of the European sovereigns are likewise wearing such helmets and armour. If Your Honour might like to see these suits of armour, a choice of them will be at your disposal at your request, while I am prepared to give Your Honour the explanations which Your Excellency might desire in person or in writing.

Also, I add to this letter a bottle of water-glass and a description for the use of this solution of glass (silicon). This liquid glass serves to protect wood and other combustibles against fire, for which they have to be painted with it.

With profound respect, I have the honour to sign, Your Excellency's servant,

(signed) Ph. F. von Siebold.

7. See Note 5.

8. ARA, Consulaat Yokohama No. 2.

Deshima, 31 December 1860

No. 514. Secret.

To the Consul General of the Netherlands in Japan.

I have the honour to send you herewith copy of a letter from the Governor of Nagasaki of the 13th of the 11th month and my answer and an exchange of letters between me and Mr von Siebold caused by this.

There was one more reason why I could not agree to Mr von Siebold's request to add to my letter to the Governor the words 'that I did not doubt that the Dutch Government would agree to let Mr von Siebold stay some time longer in Japan.'

Mr von Siebold had informed me in a conversation that we had on this matter, that he had already been making a survey at Tokitz, in order to militarily strengthen the bay on which Tokitz is situated and that he had elaborate charts in his possession of the Bay of Nagasaki for the same purpose.

I believe that the Dutch Government would not like someone like Mr von Siebold, who also has the rank of colonel at the General Staff of the Indian army, to stay in Japan to advise the Japanese Government on the building of fortifications which might be used against one of the European powers, as now and then tensions arise between some of the Treaty powers and Japan.

I have taken the liberty to offer Your Excellency my opinion as Mr von Siebold seems to have plans to propose soon to the Government plans for his staying in Japan, and this information might be of help to you.

With reference to the request of the Governor of Nagasaki, I have the honour to submit to Your Excellency to inform the Dutch Government of the desire of the Japanese Government. (Signed) The Vice Consul of the Netherlands at Nagasaki, J. P. Metman.

9. ARA, Consulaat Yokohama No. 3.

10. ARA, Consulaat Yokohama No. 3.

11. ARA, Koloniën, Geheim Verbaal No. 5923, Bijlage M.

12. ARA, Consulaat Yokohama No. 3.

13. ARA, Koloniën, Geheim Verbaal No. 5923.

[...] Already at my first audience with the Ministers of Foreign Affairs, July 10, 1861, the Minister Ando, Prince of Tsusima (he was not the governing prince of Tsusima) showed their concern about the long stay of the Russians in the Bay of Tsusima and had asked to let them know my feelings about this subject. I supposed to be able to reassure the Government that from the part of Russia they had not to fear any enmity and that the Russian flag was shown there probably because it was known that English and French warships were coming to this island to make a survey (something that really happened). Also I heard in Nagasaki and had spoken about it with the Governor, that both these great sea-powers would like to have a station on Tsusima, because this island is the most important maritime and military point in the Japanese Sea, and it governs the access to the new Russian colonies at the Tartaric Coast and the Amur. I promised to write about this matter to the Russian Admiral Likhatsoff, Commodore of the Russian Squadron in the Sea of China and Japan, whom I know well. In the meantime the Government of the Tycoon seemed to have been admonished by the English and French representatives at Edo, no longer to tolerate the presence of the Russians at Tsusima; also the English admiral Hope had been at Tsusima to tell the Russian commander to leave the island, and the Governor of Foreign Affairs, Okuli, prince of Bungo, had been ordered to go by a Japanese steamship to Tsusima to investigate the situation. Before his departure, the Government had asked me if they had the right to protest against the too long stay of the Russians in the Bay of Tsusima, to which I agreed and I remember that a protest was made up to be sent to the sovereigns of the countries which have concluded treaties with Japan.

I wrote about the affair to the admiral Likhatsoff to further a removal of the Russians from Tsusima in a peaceful way. As a result, the Commander Berileff left the harbour of Tsusima in September.[...]

14. ARA, Koloniën, Geheim Verbaal No. 5817.

15. ARA, Consulaat Yokohama No. 4.
Kanagawa, November 27, 1861.
To the Consul general of the Netherlands.
No. 173.

Some days ago, Mr von Siebold visited me to tell me officially, as he said, that he had returned from Yedo, and that he would depart for Nagasaki as soon as there would be a ship going there, but that he was not leaving Japan, and would wait for orders of the His Majesty the King to return to Yedo.

He told me that the Ministers of Foreign Affairs, at his request, had given him the reason for his dismissal, and that such had been done at your request, because they were afraid that our government would not agree with them having taken an officer in their service without permission.

However, he had got beautiful presents and the Emperor had given him a sword of honour.

The only thing I regret very much, he said, is that the Japanese Embassy will not travel in a steamship bought by the Japanese Government but will leave for Europe in the care of England in one of the British warships.

That Mr von Siebold regrets this, I can imagine, as His Honour has tried, so I have heard, to sell a steamship to the Japanese Government and as I have reported before he tried hard to accompany the Japanese Embassy to Europe. This will be ordered to the assistant at the British Legation, MacDonald.

The Consul of the Netherlands,
(signed) D. de Graeff van Polsbroek.

16. Hans Körner, Die Würzburger Siebold, p. 917.

17. ARA, Koleniën, Geheim Verbaal No. 5923. Mijne roeping door de regering van Z.M. den Taikoen, mijne verrigtingen in de hofstad en mijn ontslag door de tusschenkomst van den Consul Generaal der Nederlanden in Japan bewerkstelligd, geschied en staatkundig toegelicht en met oorkonden gestaafd. (My call by the government of H.M. the Tycoon, my acts in the residence and my dismissal brought about by the Consul General, explained and supported by documents.)

18. ARA, Yokohama 5.
Kanagawa, December 28, 1861.
To the Consul General of the Netherlands.
No. 188.

Speaking a few days ago with Mr von Siebold about the Japanese Embassy to Europe, this gentleman told me confidentially that he had advised the Japanese Government to buy the steamship *Lywoon* of the Company Dent & Company and to send the Embassy in that ship round the Cape to Europe. He had also advised to charge the ship as much as possible with silk, porcelain and lacquerware, which he wanted to sell.

Mr von Siebold changed his opinion about Japan completely and the other day, sitting at the table in the Yokohama Hotel, he has said in public 'that Japan deserved a good lesson and would receive it.' The Japanese Government has taken away the servant Sjozu from Mr von Siebold, and sent him to one of the Princes to keep him there. As you know this servant is able to speak Dutch and gave much information about Japanese affairs to Mr von Siebold.

Mr von Siebold is very angry about this and until now has, without success, tried to get his servant back.

The Consul of the Netherlands at Kanagawa,
(signed) D. de Graeff van Polsbroek.

19. ARA, Koloniën, Geheim Verbaal No. 5903.

20. ARA, Koloniën, Geheim Verbaal No. 5923. Mijne roeping, etc. Letter by von Siebold to the Governor General of the East Indies, dated Batavia, August 12, 1862.

In this letter he gives the grounds for his behaviour in Japan. Under the following point he states:

'2. It has not been my plan to enter into the service of the Tycoon, on the contrary, repeatedly I have stated to the Dutch Government, that, after the end of my call to Yedo, I wanted to be employed in a diplomatic post in Japan.

3. My purposes in accepting the call by the government to come to Yedo have been:
a). to maintain the dignity and the influence of the Netherlands in Japan
b). to favour Dutch trade and industry by the establishment of a trading agency of the Dutch Trading Company in this country.
c). To place myself as a go-between between the Japanese Government and the Representatives of the Foreign Powers to fortify the band of friendship and further the mutual trust and maintain quiet and peace in and with Japan.'

The Proprietors Assert Themselves:

The Osaka *Asahi Shinbun* and *Osaka Mainichi Shinbun* in the late nineteenth century

ALBERT A. ALTMAN

Two of present-day Japan's leading newspapers the *Asahi shinbun* and the *Mainichi shinbun*, were launched within 10 years of each other, the *Asahi* in 1879 and the *Mainichi* in 1888, and they quickly became rivals. Their financial backers came from different sections of Osaka's moneyed class; they competed for circulation and were soon to be associated with contending political parties. Nevertheless, the managerial measures they adopted to assure their viability made them organisationally similar despite these differences. It is one of these measures that is examined here.

The initial capital for the *Asahi shinbun* came from a prosperous sake brewer and wholesaler of western consumer goods, Kimura Heihachi, who established the paper for his prodigal son, Noboru. Shortly before the Restoration of 1868, Kimura had moved to Osaka where he opened a brewery. Kimura senior had gone into partnership with another wholesaler of such goods, Murayama Ryūhei, who together with Ueno Riichi became a proprietor of the paper in 1881. They put up ¥730,000 - the sum that Kimura Heihachi had already spent on the paper - Murayama ¥720,000 and Ueno ¥710,000, and the paper has remained a Murayama-Ueno property ever since.

Murayama came of a samurai family that in 1871, when the occupational restrictions on samurai employment had been lifted, had moved to Osaka where Ryūhei became a retailer of imported consumer goods.[1]

The merchant connection is also evident in the cultural milieu in which the *Asahi* took shape. It is a cliché of an inferior kind of Japanese historiography that Osaka was the centre of commerce and Tokyo of intellectual endeavour during the Meiji period; that the Osaka man was typically a merchant busy pursuing profit, while the Tokyo man, of samurai extraction, was devoted to the higher realms of thought and politics. Yet even a very cursory examination of the facts during the early years after the Restoration reveals that Osaka men, like the Osaka merchants before them in the Tokugawa period, were not disinterested in matters of the mind, any more than their samurai betters were indifferent to making money.

The *Asahi's* first manager, Kimura Noboru, for example, frequented the gatherings of a literary-cultural society, the *Shinbun Kōensha*, most of whose members were merchants. The society, which devoted itself to spreading 'culture and civilisation' like hundreds of other such societies during the Meiji period, was a meeting place of friends and, says one authority, was the city's sole cultural organisation of any influence at the time.[2] A simple listing of some of its members, their occupations and literary interests will give an impression of this coterie of what may be called *bunshō*, or 'literary merchants.'

Yamamoto Yosuke: a second-hand book-dealer and *haiku* master

Yamamoto Kansuke: a younger brother of Yosuke, also a *haiku* master

Ono Yonekichi: a rice dealer and writer of *yomimono* and *kyakuhon*

Wada Kisaburō: wholesale ship's chandler and scholar of *jōruri* texts

Ogitani Gobei: ship's chandler and writer

Nakamura Zenbei: (occupation unknown), *senryū* and *zakkai* master

Omori Kichirō: wax wholesaler, (literary interest unknown)

Tamura Futabei: proprietor of draper's shop, (literary interest unknown).

The society had a number of different links with newspapers. One of its concerns was popular education. Once a week, news stories were read out and explained to an audience that had gathered to hear short lectures on new laws, government policy and current slogans, such as *bunmei kaika* and *fukoku kyōhei*. In addition, Kōensha members prepared and distributed news stories and discursive articles free of charge to local newspapers, becoming in effect a kind of news agency at a time when such a service had not yet become common in Japan. The Tamura and Ogitani shops were collection points for news from outside the city. Tamura's son, who worked in the branch shop in Tokyo, sent news of the capital to the main shop in Osaka by fastest mail. The Ogitani shop, which sold ships' supplies and had contacts with the shipping world, had news items relayed to it by sea mail. Both shops had a clerk who made this material available to reporters who came to pick it up. Furthermore, some of the society's members were themselves regular contributors to Osaka newspapers, including the *Asahi* as soon as it came into existence on 25 January 1879.[3] The *Asahi* was the type of paper that the society's members had hoped would be published in their city: it aimed to be popular without being vulgar; it printed discursive essays and editorials, but also serialised fiction which was then a *sine qua non* for attracting large numbers of subscribers.

ATTACK ON FUJITA

The first of the interpretive pieces dealt with an event that had rocked Osaka. In December 1878, a month before the *Asahi's* first issue, counterfeit banknotes had been discovered in tax payments made in a number of localities in Kansai and suspicion had fallen on a leading Osaka figure, Fujita Denzaburō, who was a founder and head of a highly successful commercial company, the Fujitagumi, and the Chōshū clique's protégé in the city. In September 1879, Fujita and other senior company officials were suddenly arrested and taken to Tokyo for questioning. The entire affair was shrouded in secrecy apparently because of Fujita's close ties with Inoue Kaoru, a member of the government and head of the Chōshū clique, thus helping to exacerbate Chōshū-Satsuma rivalry, and a Kōensha lecture on the subject was banned by the Osaka governor on the grounds that it would endanger national security. The *Asahi* reported that it had tried unsuccessfully to get the facts at the highest levels of government in Tokyo and in the last week of September, the first of four editorials on the scandal was published under the title 'The Evil of Officials and Political Merchants Joining Hands and Doing Wrong.'[4]

In retrospect, the attack on Fujita foreshadowed the *Asahi's* rivalry with the *Mainichi*, because Fujita was one of the original investors in that paper. Unlike the proprietors of the *Asahi*, these investors occupied key positions in the Osaka business world, as the following list shows.

The six largest investors, who together provided ¥715,000, were:

Tamate Hiromichi: director of the Dojima Rice Exchange.Kanematsu Fusajirō: a member of the Exchange.Kawabara Nobuyoshi: head of the Osaka Merchant Shipping Company.Naniwa Jirōsaburō: a director of the Company.Kuwabara Shunzō: head of the Osaka branch of the Japan Construction Company, and formerly head of the Osaka government's Industrial Encouragement Department.Teramura Tomiyoshi: deputy head of the Chamber of Commerce.

The 16 others, who together provided another ¥715,000 were: Fujita Denzaburō, Kuhara Shōsaburō (Denzaburō's elder brother), Fujita Shikatarō (Denzaburō's eldest brother), Abe Hikitarō, Matsumoto Jūtarō (president of the 130th National Bank, head of the Osaka-Sakai railway and the Osaka Foreign Trade Company), Tanaka Ichibei (president of the 42nd National Bank), Kanazawa Jinbei, Kumagaya Tatsutarō (president of the 1st National Bank), Nishida Eisuke (director of the 148th National Bank) and Tsuji Chūeimon.

In the spring of 1887, Kanematsu, Kuwabara and Teramura - all members of a businessmen's club, the Dōyūkai - acquired two ailing newspapers, the *Ōsaka nippō* and the *Naniwa shinbun*, but failed to put them on sound foundations. They then approached other businessmen in the city and with the additional capital that brought the total to ¥730,000 launched the *Osaka Mainichi Shinbun* on 20 November 1888. According to one version, the immediate stimulus for publishing the paper was the poor showing of candidates backed by the business community in elections following the promulgation of the Municipal Code and Town and Village Code in April of that year. 'It all too often happened,' said one contemporary observer that 'the candidates representing the leaders of the business world lost out to men who were neither local dignitaries nor holders of real property.' The *Mainichi* was to be the voice of the solid, property-holding moneyed class in the city. Kanematsu was chosen to manage the paper on the investors' behalf and he chose as editor Shiba Shirō, who a few years earlier had published an enormously popular novel, *Kajin no kigu* (Strange Encounters of Elegant Females).[5]

CONFRONTATION WITH EDITORS

In both papers, a confrontation between the first editor and the proprietors nearly wrecked the enterprises, but in both, the proprietors gained the upper hand and established their authority. Such authority had not been the rule in most Japanese newspapers. Usually, the editor had complete control over the contents of the newspaper. Fukuchi Genichirō, one of the great pioneer journalists of the first half of the Meiji period, has described the relation between newspaper owners and their editorial writers - the *kisha* - in the 1870s, as follows:

> Newspaper proprietors took great pains to keep the *kisha* in good humour... The *kisha* were employed at so-much and so-much a month and they bore the responsibility for the paper's contents. They were not responsible for managing the newspaper and they were indifferent to it.... If the proprietor, who had invested in the paper, meddled with what was printed, they made it clear to him that it was none of his concern. 'Editing is solely our responsibility,' they would say and in no uncertain language he would be told not to interfere. If he complained, the *kisha* would threaten to leave. Sometimes, they stopped work altogether, so that the proprietor handled them gingerly. He would give them special gifts and invite them to feasts in the spring and fall. In his single-minded concentration on keeping in the good graces of the *kisha*, the proprietor behaved no differently from a theatre producer to his star actors.[6]

When the *Asahi* started coming out early in 1879, it was still commonly assumed that much of a newspaper's success depended on the literary skill of the editor and his staff. With advertising not yet an important source of revenue and news agencies not yet a significant source of domestic and foreign news, the *shuhitsu* - the 'chief brush' - wielded enormous power. He not only decided what was to be printed; the staff was responsible to him since he, not the proprietors, had hired them; very often, they had worked with him on other newspapers and accompanied him when he took up a new position. Kimura Noboru employed a well-known Osaka writer, Tsuda Takashi - he was dubbed one of the 'three talents of Naniwa' - who was also a journalist and a 'people's rights' activist.[7]

Under Tsuda's editorship, the editorial and reportorial staff of about six doubled within two months. In March, a branch office was opened in Kyoto to channel news of the city to Osaka and to handle sales; in June, another branch was opened in Kagoshima and in September, one in Tokyo. The original premises became too small for the larger, and growing, staff and for the expanded paper, and in mid-June, a move was made to roomier quarters where it was possible to install a large printing press in addition to the three smaller ones with which the *Asahi* had started. This larger press enabled the editor to increase the size of the sheet on which the paper was printed, which meant that the amount of letterpress could also be increased.

To all appearances, the *Asahi* was going from strength to strength. The initial printing run had been about 3,000 copies; by the end of June it had jumped to 4,500 and was soon approaching 7,000. But by the fall of 1879, it became clear that the editor and the proprietor were on a collision course. Despite the rising circulation, revenue was not covering expenditure. The months of October and November were hectic with attempts by Kimura Heihachi to regain control of the paper and with counter-attempts by Tsuda to maintain his authority. When Tsuda saw that he had been bested in the contest, his supporters among the editorial staff and printing workers overturned the made-up forms of type late in the afternoon of 31 May 1880, scattered the pieces of metal type on the shop floor and decamped, hoping in that way to keep the *Asahi* from appearing the following day.[8]

DEFIANCE AT *MAINICHI*

An act of defiance also occurred at the *Mainichi* in mid-May 1889. The paper was not doing well financially and the proprietors vented their frustration on Shiba, who had left himself open to attack. When he had been taken on as editor, Shiba had signed an undertaking to preserve the paper's political 'neutrality' and to develop it as an organ of Osaka business. But the proprietors were disgruntled with what they considered his lack of skill as a journalist and his disinterest in matters that concerned businessmen in Osaka. When he joined the oppositionist *Daidō danketsu* movement on whose behalf he lectured up and down the country, which took him out of the city for long stretches, and when he began publishing his partisan political views in the *Mainichi*, its owners decided to get rid of him. The opportunity came when Kanematsu decided to step down as the paper's manager, as he was moving to Kobe to look after his business interests, and recommended that the paper's finances be put on a firmer foundation. To this end, he proposed to the investors that Motoyama Hikoichi succeed him as general manager and that Motoyama install a new editor, a proposal that was accepted and to which Motoyama agreed. Motoyama had several strong marks in his favour. He had experience in journalism, having in 1883 worked on the business side of the *Ōsaka shinpō* and in the following year, 1884, joined the editorial staff of the *Jiji shinpō*, the newspaper of his mentor, Fukuzawa Yukichi, becoming as well the head of the paper's accounts department. But no doubt no less important was that in 1886 he had left the *Jiji* to become a director of the Fujitagumi and in early 1888 had married a daughter of Kuhara Shosaburō, an elder brother of Fujita Denzaburō, both of whom were investors in the *Mainichi*.

Motoyama, who remained a Fujitagumi official, then proceeded to appoint a business manager and editor. For the former, he employed Takagi Kiichirō, then business manager of the Kobe and Osaka branch offices of the *Jiji shinpō*, who had been the paper's business manager when Motoyama headed the copy desk. For editor, he chose Watanabe Osamu, then 26, who seven years earlier in 1882, when he had just graduated from Keiō, had been employed on the *Jiji shinpō* when Motoyama and Takagi were there, to take down Fukuzawa's editorials by dictation. Simultaneously, he managed another newspaper, the *Miyako*. In addition to these qualifications, Watanabe also had a literary reputation, having, while a student, translated Shakespeare, Herbert Spencer and Disraeli, and also written a biography of Bismarck.

When word of the Watanabe appointment leaked out after the *Jiji* reported it before Shiba had been informed, he and his indignant supporters among the editorial staff and printing workers retaliated by preparing an announcement for publication in the next day's issue, saying that they were quitting because the *Mainichi* stood on the verge of financial collapse. The announcement had already been set up in type when Motoyama discovered what was afoot. He hastened to inform Watanabe who had already arrived in Osaka from Tokyo. In a cliff-hanging denouement, Watanabe dashed to the *Mainichi*, had the forms of type broken up and assumed the editorial reins.[9]

PROPRIETORS ASSERT THEMSELVES

Both crises, which had been sparked by the editors and the proprietors working at cross-purposes at a time when the papers were operating at a loss, were resolved by the proprietors asserting their dominance. The new relationship with the editor meant the centralisation of control over the papers' policies, both editorial and managerial, in the hands of the owners. The editor had become their employee, albeit an intellectual one, shorn of any pretension that he had the right to fix the paper's editorial line, or to take decisions affecting the paper's management. Investments were becoming too large and competition too stiff to allow the editor to endanger the enterprise by changing the paper's viewpoint whenever he shifted his political allegiance. This change took place earlier at the *Asahi* than in other papers, giving it an important edge over the *Mainichi* in the competitive struggle in Osaka. But the proprietors' assertion of their supremacy had to be more than verbal to be effective. In both cases, at the helm stood a general manager enjoying the confidence of the proprietors (one of whom he might be, as was Murayama), who gave promise of putting the newspaper in the black in a manner that left room for further expansion, profits and influence. But the assertion of primacy over the editor was based on more than the possession of managerial skills. The *Mainichi's* proprietors, for example, did not doubt the rightness of what they were doing to accumulate their wealth. Their self-assurance as leading figures in the Osaka business community is expressed in the paper's statement of principles, which affirmed their right to speak for the entire nation. The paper would be 'neutral,' not siding with any organised political group, whether party or clique, but would take a national point of view; and the statement made clear that this point of view would be that of the propertied class in the city. The Confucian ethic that disparaged the pursuit of private profit had been turned on its head. What was good for business was now said to be good for Japan.

NOTES

1. For a more detailed account of the founding of the *Asahi*, see my 'Proprietor versus Editor: The Case of the Osaka *Asahi Shinbun* in the Late Nineteenth Century,' in *Asian and African Studies*, Vol. 14, No. 3, November 1980.
2. Fukiyoshi Torio (ed.), *Osaka no shinbun*,, Osaka, 1936, p. 41; *Ueno Riichi den*, Osaka, 1959, pp. 95-99; Shashi henshū shitsu, *Murayama Ryūhei den*, p. 96.
3. Fukuyoshi, pp. 40-46; for these men's connections with the Kaitokudō in Osaka, Miyamoto Mataji, *Miyamoto Mataji chōsakushū*, Osaka, 1979, Vol. 1, p. 507.
4. *Murayama Ryūhei den*, pp. 105-106; *Ueno Riichi den*, pp. 134-136; Takayanagi Kōji, Takeuchi Rizō (eds.), *Nihonshi jiten*, Tokyo, 1974, 'Fujitagumi gansatsu jiken,' 'Fujita Denzaburō,' pp. 820-821; *Miyamoto Mataji chōsakushū*, Vol. 1, pp. 247-252.
5. Shashi hensan iinkai, *Mainichi shinbun 70-nenshi*, Osaka, 1952, pp. 18, 20; on Tamate, *Miyamoto*, p. 281; on Kanematsu, *Miyamoto*, pp. 291-293; on Teramura, *Miyamoto*, p. 294; on Shiba and a resumé of the novel, George Sansom, *The Western World and Japan*, New York, pp. 411-415.
6. Fukuchi Genichirō, *Shinbunshi jitsureki*, (1894), reprinted in *Meiji bunka zenshū, Shinbun hen*, Tokyo, 1969, p. 13.
7. *Murayama Ryūhei den*, pp. 92-93.
8. *Murayama Ryūhei den*, pp. 95-96, 101-104.
9. *Mainichi shinbun 70-nenshi*, pp. 22-27; Ko Motoyama shachō denki hensan iinkai hensan, *Shōin Motoyama Hikoichi-ō*, Osaka, 1937, pp. 116-128, 129-130, 183-199.

The Japanese Pure Anarchists and the Theory of Anarchist-Communism

JOHN CRUMP

This paper is on the Japanese pure anarchists (*junsei museifu-shugisha*) of the 1920s and 1930s. At the outset, something needs to be said about the term 'pure anarchists.' Although the pure anarchists did on occasions use the expression 'pure anarchism,' they more often referred to themselves simply as 'anarchists' or, when they wanted to be more specific, as 'anarchist-communists.' The term 'pure anarchists' was most often used, in a sneering sense, by the opponents of the pure anarchists within the anarchist movement, that is by those anarchists who were inclined to syndicalism, the anarcho-syndicalists. In this paper I have found it convenient to use the term 'pure anarchists' as a label to identify this current in Japanese anarchism, but in so doing I have stripped the term of its abusive connotations so that I use it entirely neutrally. I prefer not to follow the pure anarchists and call them anarchist-communists because I want to reserve this latter term for all anarchist-communists, not merely in Japan but throughout the world. Thus if I use the term 'pure anarchists' it enables me to distinguish the particular Japanese species of a wider genus which includes, for example, the great Russian theoretician of anarchist-communism, Peter Kropotkin. However, I do refer to the ideology of the pure anarchists as anarchist-communism, since that ideology had so much in common with Kropotkin's theories and, indeed, in the shape it was given by the foremost theoretician among the pure anarchists, Hatta Shūzō, was a creative development of many of Kropotkin's core ideas.

This paper is divided into five sections, the first four of which are brief and provide a background for the substantial discussion of pure anarchist theory in Section 5. Section 1 argues that conventional accounts of anarchism in Japan are misleading, implying that it went into catastrophic decline, both organisationally and intellectually, after Ōsugi Sakae's murder in 1923. Section 2 sketches the historical development of Japanese anarchism prior to the 1920s and 1930s. Section 3 looks at the growth of trade unions in Japan, since it was the question of trade union strategy which was the principal issue that divided pure anarchists from anarcho-syndicalists. Section 4 summarises the key concepts of anarchist-communism as developed by the person who played the dominant role in elaborating its theory until his death in 1921, Peter Kropotkin. Finally, Section 5 introduces the foremost theoretician of anarchist-communism in Japan, the pure anarchist Hatta Shūzō, and discusses the ways in which he pushed the theoretical frontiers of anarchist-communism beyond the points at which they had been left by Kropotkin.

1. CONVENTIONAL ACCOUNTS OF ANARCHISM IN JAPAN

In George M. Beckmann's and Ōkubo Genji's *The Japanese Communist Party 1922-1945*, we find the comment:

> In the view of many Japanese historians and commentators, Osugi's murder symbolises the end of anarchism as an important force in Japanese intellectual circles, and in the labour movement.[1]

This coincides with Robert Scalapino's assessment that 'the Sōdōmei (Japanese Federation of Labour) convention of October 1922... signalled the end of anarchist power in the Japanese labour movement' and that, after Ōsugi's murder, anarchism commanded no more than 'isolated intellectual support.'[2] Thomas A. Stanley in his biography of Ōsugi Sakae goes even further than this, in that he asserts that 'Ōsugi's death is virtually an insignificant accident' since 'anarchism was much eclipsed' even before that event.[3]

In Section 3 I will show that these death certificates on the anarchist labour movement in the early 1920s are premature. Anarchist trade unions continued to attract a by no means negligible body of support until the general collapse of trade unionism due to the increasing intensity of state repression in the 1930s. As for the intellectual vitality of anarchism in Japan, the following comments by Ōta Ryū certainly convey an impression that is different from the conventional accounts:

> Hatta Shūzō (born 1886; died 1934) was an important anarchist after the murder of Ōsugi Sakae (in 1923). Basing himself on Kropotkinism, he developed the theory of anarchist-communism one step further. After Kropotkin's death, world anarchism rapidly regressed from the level that Kropotkin had brought it to. It seems to me that, as far as I know, in the midst of these degenerate circumstances (the era of Marxism-Leninism's complete domination) there was nobody other than Hatta (not only in Japan but in the entire world) who took a step forward in this way.
>
> To correctly appreciate Hatta's achievement, to study his work and develop it further, is now an extremely important theoretical task.[4]

2. HISTORICAL DEVELOPMENT OF JAPANESE ANARCHISM PRIOR TO THE 1920s

It is an arbitrary decision where one locates the historical origins of anarchism in Japan. For the purposes of this paper, it is convenient to see Japanese anarchism as originating during the period 1906-18, but we should not forget that the *Nihon Heimin Shinbun* for 20 January 1908 carried an article on 'Andō Shōeki: an Anarchist of 150 Years Ago.'[5] A more recent book on Japanese anarchism, the Libertaire Group's *A Short History of the Anarchist Movement in Japan*, refers to Andō as 'a forerunner of anarchism' and points out that Andō lived 'a century-and-a-half before Proudhon, Bakunin and

Marx had appeared in the world history. He denounced the feudal moral education and advocated the agricultural communist anarchism.'[6] Nevertheless, in this paper I do not wish to go back any further than the period 1906-18 and I want to argue that, although for practical purposes Japanese anarchism at this time amounted to an imported western doctrine, it struck a cord with trends which were occurring within Japan. As a doctrine of direct action, anarchism corresponded with the experiences of spirited sections of the Japanese working class and peasantry (such as the miners of Ashio and the rice rioters of Toyama) who, driven to desperate lengths by their poverty and the oppression which they suffered, were forced into direct physical confrontation with the forces of the state. Key influences which acted on the Japanese socialists of this period and led many of them towards anarchism were Kōtoku Shūsui's visit to the USA in 1905-6 and his subsequent declaration 'The Change in My Thought,' which appeared as an article in the *Heimin Shinbun* on 5 February 1907; inspiration derived from the activist role of the SRs within Russia and from the Russian exile, Peter Kropotkin's anarchist-communist writings, such as *The Conquest of Bread* (which was translated into Japanese in 1909); and the lessons that were drawn from the development of syndicalist unions, in France and elsewhere, which advocated the strategy of 'The Social General Strike' (the title of an influential pamphlet by Arnold Roller that was translated into Japanese in 1907).

Both anarchist-communist and syndicalist influences were thus evident within Japanese anarchism in this period and, as is well known, in contemporary Europe there was a discernible tension between these two anarchist tendencies. At the international anarchist conference held in Amsterdam in August 1907, for example, there was a debate between Pierre Monatte of the French syndicalist federation, the CGT, and the Italian anarchist, Errico Malatesta. Monatte was naturally heavily committed to the trade unions and the strategy of the general strike, while Malatesta neither shared the anarcho-syndicalists' faith that the unions represented *the* means of revolution nor did he see the unions as the elements from which a new society could be constructed. What lay behind Malatesta's uneasiness with the syndicalist approach was the contradiction which he sensed existed between the mass of trade unionists, engaged in day-to-day skirmishing *within* capitalism, and the handfuls of revolutionaries, dreaming of a new society *beyond* capitalism.

As I made clear in *The Origins of Socialist Thought in Japan*, 'Tension between anarcho-syndicalists and "pure" anarchists did not develop in earnest in Japan until after the period extending up to 1918.... This was obviously because there was no trade union movement worth talking of in Japan throughout most of this period, the handfuls of revolutionaries having the field to themselves.'[7] In European countries, such as France, where there were both well established anarchist movements and sizeable syndicalist federations, friction had developed because the interests of anarchists and syndicalists were often opposed. Just how different conditions were in Japan prior to 1918 is revealed by Ōsugi Sakae's bland comments, made in October 1914, which show how divorced those like Ōsugi were from the problem:

> A long way away as we are, we can look calmly at the relationship between both parties. And it seems to us that the inevitable tendency in both cases should be for anarchists to become trade unionists and for trade unionists to become anarchists, so that in the end there is perfect agreement between them. The vague abstract theories of Kropotkin and others have become clear and concrete in the trade unions. And the trade unions, which for a long time have been weak and uncertain of themselves, have learned through experience and, thanks to anarchism, are at last marching straight ahead in a definite direction.[8]

That things were not as simple as Ōsugi imagined, and that the cracks between pure anarchists and anarcho-syndicalists could not easily be papered over, became clear subsequently after a trade union movement developed within Japan.

3. TRADE UNIONS AND ANARCHISM IN JAPAN

The *chian keisatsu hō* (public peace police law) had in effect outlawed trade unions when it was introduced in 1900. From then on, any attempts at trade union organisation were suppressed until the *Yūaikai* (Friendship Society) was formed by Suzuki Bunji and others in 1912. The *Yūaikai* owed its survival as much to the fact that its 'policy was to recommend conciliation between labour and capital whenever disputes occurred' as it did to having 'scholars, social reformers and capitalists' on its executive council.[9] Yet, despite this unpromising start, in retrospect the *Yūaikai* can be seen as the trade unions' foot in the door of Japanese capitalism. Already by the middle of the *Taishō* era the *Yūaikai's* membership had grown to about 30,000 and subsequently the trade union movement came to extend far beyond the ranks of the *Yūaikai* and its *Sōdōmei* successor. Hagiwara Shintarō records that there were 103,000 trade unionists organised in 300 unions in 1921, 254,000 in 457 unions in 1925, and 331,000 in 630 unions in 1929.[10]

Broadly speaking, this union movement attracted the organisational efforts of three types of activist - social-democratic, Communist Party (after the formation of the Communist Party in 1922) and anarchist. The fact that the percentage of unions under anarchist influence declined from the early 1920s is taken as evidence that the anarchists lost out to the social-democrats and the Communist Party, but two important qualifications need to be made. Firstly, anarchist influence persisted. Relatively, the anarchists may have given ground, but an organised anarchist presence within the union movement remained. Secondly, conventional trade unionism (in its anarchist form, syndicalism) came under increasingly outspoken attack from within the anarchist movement. This was not simply a case of anarchists rationalising their losses and declaring, like bad-tempered children, that they did not want what had been taken from them. On the contrary, it was rather a case of theoretical innovation by the pure anarchists.

To illustrate the former point, we can take the founding conference of the *Zenkoku Rōdō Kumiai Jiyū Rengōkai* (the All-Japan Libertarian Federation of Labour Unions - *Zenkoku Jiren* for short) which was held in Tokyo on 24 May 1926. Attended by some 400 delegates, representing 8,372 workers from 25 unions, *Zenkoku Jiren* was the anarchist answer to the social-democratic *Sōdōmei* and the Communist Party's *Hyōgikai* union federations. Compared to its social-democratic and Communist Party rivals, its distinguishing policy decisions were its complete opposition to all political movements and its determination to propagate the idea of free federation (*jiyū rengōshugi*) among the workers. However, *Zenkoku Jiren's* fate also serves to illustrate the second point. Soon after its formation, the pure anarchists, who were opposed to adopting a syndicalist strategy, put their stamp on the organisation. By virtue of their majority within *Zenkoku Jiren's* ranks, they were able to give the federation an unmistakably pure anarchist orientation and this provoked the anarcho-syndicalist minority to break away in 1928. The following year the anarcho-sydicalists established a rival union federation, the *Nihon Rōdō Kumiai Jiyū Rengō Kyōgikai* (the Japanese Libertarian United Conference of Labour Unions - *Nihon Jikyō* for short).

In pre-war Japan the highest rate of trade union organisation that was achieved was 7.9 per cent of the workforce (369,000 members) in 1931. In the same year *Zenkoku Jiren's* membership had grown to 16,300, while the recently formed *Nihon Jikyō* had 3,000 members. Together, this gave the anarchist-affiliated trade unions of both complexions a combined membership of 19,300 in 1931. While this was a mere 5 per cent of all trade unionists in Japan, it was nevertheless a not entirely negligible fraction of the organised labour force, particularly in view of the fact that the anarchists' militancy partially compensated for what they lacked in numbers. However, by 1932 Japan was perceptibly sliding into military rule at home and towards full-scale war abroad. All organisations opposed to these trends were under intense pressure and, not surprisingly, both *Zenkoku Jiren* and *Nihon Jikyō* saw their membership contract from then on. In a desperate attempt to withstand state oppression, both union federations suppressed their differences sufficiently to reunite in 1934 behind the *Zenkoku Jiren* banner, but by 1935 total membership was down to 2,300. As Komatsu Ryūji has put it, 'from November 1935, the nationwide arrests of anarchists began' and as 'the round-up of the remaining anarchists went ahead' in 1936, *Zenkoku Jiren* was disbanded.[11]

The formation of *Zenkoku Jiren* in 1926 thus brought into the open differences among the anarchists which had hitherto lain dormant. For a brief period during the late 1920s and early 1930s these differences provoked an intense theoretical debate between rival anarchist currents and a consequent flowering of anarchist thought. The controversy was not settled by the free expression of ideas, however, but was extinguished by the repressive actions of the Japanese state.

KROPOTKIN'S ANARCHIST-COMMUNISM

When the pure anarchists appeared in Japan at the beginning of the *Shōwa* era, the anarchist-communist doctrine with which they identified was that which had been elaborated by Peter Kropotkin during the four decades from his conversion to anarchist-communism in the 1880s until his death in 1921. The principal features of this doctrine were as follows:

Kropotkin stood for the achievement of an anarchist-communist society whose communist aspect signified communal living, communal production and the fact that the community would be supportive of individuals, while its anarchist aspect signified that individuals would be free, unoppressed by any state, and able to pursue their physical, emotional, artistic and scientific aspirations within the unrestrictive framework provided by the community. Once the land and the other means of production had been expropriated from their private owners, argued Kropotkin, resources would be sufficient to ensure well-being for all. It was not communal ownership as such that would bring about plenty, but rather the spirit of voluntary, communal work that would unleash abundance. As Kropotkin asserted:

> [Compared to a hired worker], a free worker, who sees ease and luxury increasing for him and for others in proportion to his efforts, spends infinitely far more energy and intelligence, and obtains first-class products in a far greater abundance.[12]

The unit of social organisation was to be the autonomous commune, which would be freely federated with other communes, and the principle to be followed when distributing goods within the commune was 'no stint or limit to what the community possesses in abundance, but equal sharing and dividing of those things which are scarce or apt to run short.'[13] The communes would spell the end of the division of labour, which Kropotkin regarded as bad for society but even worse for the individual. Kropotkin was against occupational specialisation and economic concentration, and recommended instead decentralised 'industrial villages' (a synonym for the free communes) which would ensure a mixture of trades and productive activities in all localities. One consequence of reorganising society in this fashion would be the abolition of the distinction between town and country, since science would be available to the rural communes and agriculture would spread into the former towns. Even more important, however, would be the consequences for the individual. There would be no more 'separation between manual work and brain work,' since labour would involve 'the free exercise of *all* the faculties of man,' the 'combination of agriculture and industry, the husbandman and the mechanic in the same individual.'[14] Similarly, communal living and the grass roots application of science and technology would liberate women from domestic toil.[15]

Kropotkin regarded anarchist-communism not merely as desirable but as a form of social organisation which came naturally to men and women. He saw mutual aid as 'a law of Nature and chief factor of progressive evolution,' so that the achievement of anarchist-communism would not be so much a step forward as a return to the type of social relations by means of which humankind had prospered throughout most of its history.[16] In Kropotkin's view, all that was required for humankind to retrieve its natural harmony was for the people to rise in insurrection, throw off their oppressors and vow to themselves that never again would they be ruled.

HATTA SHŪZŌ'S ANARCHIST-COMMUNISM

For the impoverished villagers, poor peasants and tenant farmers of early *Shōwa* Japan, Kropotkin's description of anarchist-communism must have sounded like paradise. Hence not only did the pure anarchists devote their efforts to *Zenkoku Jiren* and the industrial workers, but they recognised the potential for building support in the agricultural communities. Frequent propaganda tours of farming districts were organised and none was keener to spread the word than the heavy drinking, lapsed priest, Hatta Shūzō.

Hatta Shūzō was born in 1886 and died in 1934. His early intellectual development was not promising, in that he was converted to Christianity and became a clergyman after graduating from college in 1912. A developing interest in anarchism, coupled with disillusionment with Christianity, led to his expulsion from his church and, after moving to Tokyo in 1924, for the next 10 years he devoted himself to anarchist activity and became a prominent speaker and writer in the anarchist movement. Despite his 'gentlemanly' appearance, Hatta was a fiery speaker and incisive writer and years later his comrade Daidōji Saburō recalled what it was like to visit his home village with Hatta. Whereas the police invariably intervened at *Zenkoku Jiren* meetings in the cities, they rarely intruded into the farming hamlets, so that 60 members of Daidōji's village were able to gather to listen to Hatta speak. In his recollections, Daidōji recalled how pictures of Kropotkin and the Ukrainian anarchist guerrilla, Nestor Makhno, decorated the room and also the electric atmosphere that Hatta was able to conjure up. On the evening of their arrival and the following night too, Hatta spoke from early evening until midnight for five or six hours at a stretch without stopping. The audience was riveted. Nobody dozed off and many of the women were moved to tears. The atmosphere within the room, recalled Daidōji, was 'like the eve of the revolution.'[17]

It was in the course of this intensive propaganda work, both spoken and written, in the late 1920s and early 1930s that Hatta built on Kropotkin's ideas and established the reputation of being 'the greatest theoretician of anarchist-communism in Japan.'[18] In the remainder of this paper I want to discuss: (a) the major themes that Hatta introduced into anarchist-communism; and (b) those themes already present in Kropotkin's writings which Hatta developed significantly further.

To take first the new themes which Hatta introduced into Kropotkin's anarchist-communism, these were:

(i) his outright rejection of syndicalism;
(ii) his criticism of the *soviet* (council) form of organisation;
(iii) his opposition to the theory of the class struggle;
(iv) his advocacy of vanguardism.

(1) *Syndicalism* Kropotkin's attitude towards syndicalism had been ambivalent, whereas Hatta rejected syndicalism unequivocally.[19] Hatta took up the issue of syndicalism in some of his best known texts and his pamphlet *Sanjikarizumu no Kentō* (*An Examination of Syndicalism*) in particular exerted a major influence on the anarchist movement in Japan. Hatta regarded syndicalism not primarily as an ideology in its own right but rather as a 'tendency within the labour movement' which had emerged as a reaction to political opportunism. However, syndicalists had found it necessary to explain their actions by reference to theories and ideology and, in Hatta's view, they had done this by drawing on both anarchism and Marxism in an attempt to create a hybrid out of them:

> ...since syndicalism is not itself a specific ideology, it underpins itself with some other ideology. And in answer to the question what is it that ideologically underpins syndicalism, I can only conclude that it is a combination of Marxism and anarchism. In other words, syndicalism can be said to be, in this sense, a hybrid creature.[20]

Since Hatta considered anarchism and Marxism to be opposed fundamentally (both politically and philosophically) he believed that syndicalism was inherently unstable and that syndicalists would show a tendency to gravitate towards one or other of the opposing ideologies from which they derived their contradictory ideas. Furthermore, since syndicalists had taken so many of their key ideas (such as the theory of the class struggle) from Marxism, Hatta believed they were more likely to gravitate towards it than towards anarchism.

An additional reason for rejecting syndicalism was that it accepted the division of labour within society. Hatta' reasons for denouncing any form of social organisation which entailed the division of labour will be explained below. Here I shall merely outline his specific criticism of syndicalism within the context of his general opposition to the social division of labour. As Hatta saw it, by basing its organisation on *syndicats* (unions) which were themselves a product of capitalism's division of labour, and by intending to carry over this *syndicat*-based organisational structure into post-revolutionary society, syndicalism would have the effect of perpetuating the division of labour and the power structure which, he believed, derived from it. He argued:

> syndicalism will take over, just as it is (*sono mama*), the capitalist mode of production and perpetuate the system of big factories, the division of labour system and the economic organisation that takes production as its basis.[21]

In other words since the *syndicats* emerged within a workforce engaged in capitalist production, they constituted a movement whose organisation was automatically a mirror-image of the industrial structure generated by capitalism, including the social division of labour. Hence, far from syndicalism being able to solve the problems inherent in capitalism, such as the social division of labour, it and capitalism (and Bolshevik-style 'communism' too, added Hatta) were all 'cut from the same cloth.'[22]

(ii) *Soviets* Hatta's criticisms of plans for reorganising society on the basis of *soviets* (workers' councils) overlapped his arguments against syndicalism. For that reason, his denunciation of *soviets* and of syndicalism often accompanied one another.[23] Here, again, Hatta's position contrasted with Kropotkin's, since Kropotkin had evaluated the *soviets* positively when they first appeared in the Russian revolution of 1905 and had continued to do so until the end of his life, idealising them as organs of struggle and of free discussion and deploring their fate when, after 1917, they fell under Bolshevik control.[24] For his part, Hatta opposed *soviets*, as he did *syndicats*, because he regarded them as organisations based on the division of labour, which would therefore perpetuate power relationships. Since both on their first appearance in 1905 and on later occasions too, *soviets* had emerged spontaneously within factories and other places of employment, Hatta argued that, just like the *syndicats*, they reflected the social division of labour that was inherent in capitalism's system of industrial organisation:

> The *soviets* are a machinery of administration which arises because the working class, as the producers, control society. Those who seek to establish *soviets* insist that it is the system of production based on the division of labour which becomes the basis of society...[25]

Like Kropotkin, Hatta denounced the 'party *soviets*' of the Bolsheviks as organs of state power. However, Hatta went further than Kropotkin, maintaining that even in the case of 'free *soviets*' or 'class *soviets*' some would have more power than others. His line of reasoning was that, since *soviets* of all types were based on production, any members of society who were not currently taking part in production would be disadvantaged in a *soviet* system. Likewise, those who were engaged in vital lines of production would have more power than those engaged in more peripheral sectors. Thus he argued:

> ...however, purely economic the *soviets* might be, the reason is obvious why the building of them will be accompanied by the emergence of power.[26]

It was for reasons such as these that Hatta criticised anarchists who sought to compromise on the question of *soviets*. He wrote:

> What deluded the Russian anarchists at the time of the revolution was this word *soviet*. Those like [Alexander] Berkman, using the expression 'free *soviet*,' even tried to introduce sovietism (*sobietoshugi*) into anarchism.[27]

(iii) *Class Struggle* Syndicalists saw revolution as the culmination of a developing class struggle within capitalism, but Hatta emphasised that for him class struggle and revolution were 'two entirely different things.' In an article entitled *Sanjikarizumu ni tai suru Ichi Kōsatsu* ('An Enquiry into Syndicalism' which he wrote for *Kokushoku Seinen* (*Black Youth*) in 1927, he asserted:

> Syndicalism says that it will bring about the revolution by means of the class struggle, but that is a major mistake. The class struggle and the revolution are two opposing movements; one does not give birth to the other.[28]

Hatta considered reliance on the class struggle to be flawed both in terms of method and of goal. Classes struggle over mundane issues in a process which is characterised by advances and retreats. Not only is any progress that is registered slow and incremental, but the tactics employed by one class are inevitably transferred to another. One can convey Hatta's thinking on this last point by using the analogy of a boxing match. In the ring, both boxers use similar techniques (uppercuts, feints, jabs and so on) and, if one boxer develops a new technique, his rival is forced to follow suit if he is to stand any chance of winning the bout. It is the same with the class struggle. One class is forced to adopt the techniques employed by its rival and, since the capitalist class makes use of state power, the working class inevitably becomes ensnared in attempts to erect its 'own' state. Even if the class struggle is fought to an apparently successful conclusion, the victory of the oppressed class merely signifies a reversal of positions, a new system of class domination, not an end to class divisions.

By way of contrast, Hatta saw revolution as a once-and-for-all, life-and-death explosion that transcends the structures of the old society, including classes. Its methods are different from those employed in the class struggle because it does not base itself on what exists within capitalism (industrial disputes, campaigns for reform and so on). Although revolution can be prepared for, it does not progress gradually and incrementally as does the class struggle. Similarly, the goal of the revolution can only be the destruction of the old order and the rebuilding of society on an entirely different basis, not a re-arrangement of the existing pieces (classes, industries etc.) of the capitalist jigsaw, as the exponents of class struggle envisage.

Not only did Hatta reject the methods and goal of the class struggle, but he also questioned the concept of social class which syndicalists and Marxists employed. Both syndicalists and Marxists habitually focused their attention on what they saw as the two principal classes in modern society - the capitalists and the proletariat. Polarising society in this fashion, they regularly consigned all sorts of poverty-stricken strata into the 'proletariat,' irrespective of whether they were workers (*rōdōsha*), small traders, petty officials (*yakuba no kozukai*) or belonged to other social groups. In opposition to this inaccurate method of class analysis, which pitchforked a variety of disparate elements into the proletariat (*musan kaikyū*), Hatta favoured the concept of the 'propertyless masses' (*musan taishū*). Besides the strata already mentioned above, the 'propertyless masses' might include tenant farmers, lumpens, alienated intellectuals and so forth. In Hatta's opinion, here was another reason why the pure anarchists should not base themselves on the class struggle. The 'propertyless masses' were not confined to a single class and therefore class struggle was not an appropriate means of achieving their emancipation. Some other term was required to express the means by which the 'propertyless masses' could emancipate themselves. To Hatta it was clear that this term should be 'revolutionary action.' The following quotation neatly summarises this area of Hatta's thought:

> If ...we understand that the proletariat (*musan kaikyū*) and the propertyless masses (*musan taishū*) are different things, and that the class struggle and the revolution are different things, then we are forced to say that it is a major mistake to declare, as the syndicalists do, that the revolution will be brought about by the class struggle. Even if a change in society came about by means of the class struggle, it would not mean that a genuine revolution had occurred.[29]

(iv) *Vanguardism* Kropotkin had rejected the theory and the practice of vanguardism, of the revolution being initiated by an activist minority.[30] In general, Hatta had enormous respect for Kropotkin and he regarded his ability as a theoretician as far superior to that of other anarchist thinkers, such as Proudhon and Bakunin.[31] Nevertheless, Hatta appreciated Bakunin's rebellious spirit and his philosophy of violence and it was these characteristics that induced him to describe Bakunin as a 'giant' and a 'titan.'[32] Hatta introduced vanguardism into anarchist-communism and it seems that his inclination towards minority action derived from other strains of anarchism, such as Bakuninism.

Hatta favoured 'creative violence by a minority' and one of his subsidiary arguments against the pure anarchists embracing the class struggle was that this would involve basing themselves on majority action, which would be bound to have a damping effect on the revolutionary spirit of the minority and ultimately transform them into reformists.[33] It was implicit in Hatta's vision of an anarchist-communist society that, in order to achieve such a state of affairs, the 'propertyless masses' would have to emancipate themselves. As we have seen, Hatta's concept of 'propertyless masses' was so all-embracing as clearly to encompass a majority of the population. Nevertheless, Hatta had no quarrel with the idea that 'true liberation for the workers will be brought about by the heroic and creative initiative of a minority of conscious activists arousing the majority.'[34] Although Hatta did not envisage that an élite would seize power (and even less did he imagine that a group would exercise control after the revolution) he was still a vanguardist in the sense of expecting the revolutionary explosion of the masses to be detonated by a committed minority.

Turning to those themes already present in Kropotkin's theory of anarchist-communism which Hatta developed further, the following are worthy of attention:

> (1) opposition to Marxism; (ii) opposition to the division of
> labour and seeking to transcend this by means of the
> autonomous commune/cooperative village; (iii) advocacy of
> free association; (iv) rejection of the transitional period.

(1) *Marxism*   In a far more systematic fashion than Kropotkin, Hatta
took issue with the key components of Marxist theory - the theory of
the class struggle, the labour theory of value and the materialist
conception of history. His arguments against the theory of the class
struggle have already been examined. Although Hatta primarily
identified the labour theory of value with Marxism, he did concede that
anarchists such as Proudhon and Bakunin had also subscribed to
versions of this theory. In Hatta's opinion, it was one of Kropotkin's
greatest achievements to have broken with these earlier strains of
anarchism and to have abandoned the labour theory of value. Hatta
did not dispute the usefulness of the labour theory of value for analysing
the workings of capitalism, but he argued that any attempt to preserve
exchange value and labour-time calculation in a communist society
would prove disastrous. Marx had toyed with such ideas when
developing his concept of 'the first phase of communist society' in *The
Critique of the Gotha Programme*[35] and, in *The Conquest of Bread*,
Kropotkin had pertinently criticised Marx and his followers for precisely
this reason.[36] Hatta upheld this criticism, insisting that:

> When labour becomes the basis of all value, we are destroying the
> foundation of the concept of communism.[37]

As for the materialist conception of history, Hatta rejected Marx's
notion of historical progression and also his concept of capitalism. For
Hatta, capitalism was not a social system based on the relationship
between wage labour and capital which was historically progressive
relative to feudalism. Hatta saw capitalism as any society based on
private property and exploitation, including the class societies of ancient
history:

> Capitalism is not simply the wages system. That being the case,
> capitalism existed in any number of eras. All exploitative economic
> systems that arise from the private ownership of capital are
> capitalism; it is not simply the one means of exploitation that takes
> the form of the wages system that is capitalism. In the history of
> humankind, capitalism has recurred again and again since ancient
> times.[38]

In accordance with this view, there was no progress in human history,
but a perpetual ebbing and flowing of capitalism and centralised rule
on the one hand and the decentralised, communal villages on the other.
In periods when capitalism and government were on the ascendant,
common ownership and liberty went into decline, and vice versa.

Hatta objected to the Marxist notion of dialectical historical
progression on the grounds that this gave a measure of legitimacy to

whatever existed. Dismissing dialectics, Hatta advocated what he called a 'principle of action,' according to which men and women were not constrained by the historical epoch in which they lived but were at liberty in any era to reject whatever they found oppressive and to struggle for whatever they believed in. 'History does not repeat itself, nor does it progress' Hatta asserted. What history did provide evidence of, however, was the people's 'strong will for liberty - a will to live - which government and exploitation cannot destroy.' On this reading of history, anarchist-communism would not be the outcome of a historical process, but a historical breakthrough brought about by a triumph of the human will to live freely. With the type of misplaced optimism that Kropotkin was also famous for, Hatta claimed that 'the day is close' and that 'final victory is not far off.'[39]

(ii) *The Division of Labour*   As with Kropotkin, Hatta considered the elimination of the division of labour as crucial to the success of anarchist-communism. By 'division of labour' (*bungyō*) he did not mean a mere 'division of work' (*tewake*). Even within an anarchist-communist society he anticipated that, at any one time, different people would be engaged in different jobs:

> It goes without saying that whatever the kind of production, there has to be a division of work (*tewake*) within society.[40]

What characterised the division of labour was geographical or sectional specialisation. This could take the form of industry being concentrated in certain zones and agriculture elsewhere, or it might present as the workforce being organised according to specialised occupations (steel workers, textile workers and so forth).

In his pamphlet *Sanjikarizumu no Kentō*, Hatta argued that such economic specialisation produced a number of effects. Firstly, when people are confined to the endless repetition of the same specialised operations, 'labour is made mechanical.' Secondly, it results in a situation where those involved in one branch of production have 'neither responsibility for, understanding of, nor interest in' other branches of production. Thirdly, in order to coordinate the various branches of production, a 'superior coordinating machinery' arises, which is in the hands of a social group that does not itself engage in production. Hatta insisted that 'it is beyond doubt that power will arise within such a group.'[41] Elsewhere Hatta asserted that a further effect of the division of labour is that the products of different economic sectors are exchanged on the basis of value. Hence, according to Hatta, exchange relations and power relations could all ultimately be traced back to the division of labour as their root cause:

> Where the division of labour occurs, exchange takes place. Where exchange takes place, a medium of exchange - in other words, money (or labour vouchers) - comes into existence. And money stands in need of a basis of centralised power (government).[42]

In order to transcend the division of labour and its consequences, Hatta advocated reorganising society as a federation of autonomous communes or cooperative villages. Since most production would then take place on the limited scale of the decentralised commune, people would not be alienated from one another even when they engaged in different productive activities. Similarly, the need for a 'superior coordinating machinery' would be eliminated because detailed information on local resources and local needs would be common knowledge, ensuring that everyone had the necessary know-how to participate in decision-making and coordination. Since Hatta expected all members of the local commune to take part both in production and in coordinating activity and decision-making, he was confident that there would be no possibility for groups wielding power to emerge. In such a decentralised system, production would be for the sole purpose of satisfying people's consumption needs, resulting in 'an economic organisation which takes consumption as its basis.' Hatta contrasted this arrangement with the way in which consumption needs are eclipsed by production considerations in a system that incorporates the division of labour, which is therefore 'an economic organisation which takes production as its basis.'[43]

(iii) *Free Association*   Hatta was a passionate advocate of 'free association' (*jiyū rengōshugi*). Like Kropotkin in *Mutual Aid*, Hatta believed that free association was not just a good idea or one among a number of contending theories of social organisation. Rather it was a natural characteristic of human beings, a fundamental truth or principle which we all recognise from our experience of life, knowing that without it life would simply collapse and we ourselves would perish. It was for this reason that Hatta opposed those anarchists who suggested that anarchism needed a theory of organisation to rival the so-called 'democratic centralism' of the Bolsheviks.

In an article entitled *Warera no Susumu beki Michi* ('The Road That We Should Advance Along') which first appeared in *Kurohata* (*Black Flag*) in January 1930, Hatta argued strongly against attempting artificially to 'organise' the anarchist movement or pursuing a particular mode of organisation. Hatta's argument was that there are two basic forms of organisation, 'natural (*shizenteki*) organisation' and 'artificial (*jin'iteki*) organisation.' Anarchism should base itself on 'natural organisation, which is not something that has to be striven for, since it comes into existence as a matter of course. By way of contrast, 'artificial organisation is inevitably accompanied by power and coercion' and it therefore followed that 'what we are opposed to is this form of organisation.'[44] For Hatta, any deficiencies that anarchism might exhibit do not arise from its lack of organisation. On the contrary, for him anarchism's distinctive strength lay in the fact that it does not resort to 'artificial organisation,' but relies instead on free association. The role of the pure anarchists was thus defined by Hatta as essentially propagandistic (including 'propaganda by the deed'). The pure anarchists had an explanatory role to fulfil, but their activity did not extend into the sphere of organising other people:

If we just earnestly grasp anarchism and explain it, we can leave it to other people to come together freely, according to their various interests and inclinations. A naturally evolving organisation based on free association will then be born (*it will not be made*). There is no need to organise people and create structures for them, all the while prattling on about organisation.[45]

(iv) *The Transitional Period*   Hatta rejected the idea of a revolutionary transitional period which would act as a prelude to full-scale anarchist-communism. According to him, those who countenance a transitional period, no matter how well intentioned they might be, envisage the continuation of the division of labour and 'also think that during the transitional period it should be the working class that necessarily controls society.'[46] Hatta pointed out that this was a key element in the thinking of both syndicalists and advocates of *soviets* (workers' councils) and that they were completely mistaken. The notion of a transitional period involved using elements of capitalism supposedly in order to put an end to capitalism. Those who thought along such lines were fostering illusions:

> This kind of transitional period is an extension of capitalism. It is a case of trying to advance by means of the basic principles of capitalism, principles such as having a state based on centralised power and a mode of production based on the division of labour. Due to this, it means becoming ensnared in the same sort of contradiction as one who talks about 'becoming a thief in order to stop being a thief'... The sham called the transitional period is something which only cowards intent on deceiving the masses could think of.[47]

Hatta believed that to allow the division of labour to continue after the revolution (albeit 'temporarily') and to entertain the notion of a 'transitional state' could only mean that the outcome would be much the same as Bolshevik rule in Russia. In fact, for Hatta the Russian experience provided the best example of the dangers of thinking in terms of a transitional period. He seems to have believed that the events of 1917 had opened up virtually unlimited possibilities in Russia, but that these were squandered precisely because the revolution was harnessed to the 'transitional' aims of the Bolsheviks. In 1926 he wrote that 'if Lenin had adopted the ideas of Kropotkin and had advanced to a multiform system of decentralised production,' it would not have been necessary for Russia to have 'reverted to capitalism.'[48] In Hatta's view, the division of labour and the rule of government have to be abolished immediately and human creativity allowed to flourish within the autonomous communes that will arise at the very outset of an anarcho-communist revolution. Any postponing of these changes can only spell doom. In that sense, he was echoing Kropotkin's prognosis that 'the Revolution must be communist or it will be drowned in blood.'[49]

What this paper has sought to demonstrate is that Hatta Shūzō was an anarchist-communist theoretician of considerable originality and importance. The fact that he was able to push the theoretical frontiers of anarchist-communism beyond the points at which they had been left by Peter Kropotkin cannot be explained, however, simply by reference to the force of his personality or to his ability as a thinker. Rather, the ideas to which he gave theoretical expression emerged out of the confrontation between pure anarchists and anarcho-syndicalists which divided the anarchist movement in Japan in the late 1920s and early 1930s.

NOTES

1. George M. Beckmann and Ōkubo Genji, *The Japanese Communist Party 1922-1945* (Stanford, 1969) p. 71.
2. Robert A. Scalapino, *The Japanese Communist Movement 1920-1966* (Berkeley and Los Angeles, 1967) p. 14.
3. Thomas A. Stanley *Ōsugi Sakae: Anarchist in Taishō Japan* (Cambridge, Mass., 1982) pp. 160-1.
4. Ōta Ryū, 'Anakizumu Ron' ('On Anarchism') in Ōshima Seizaburō (ed.) *Museifukyōsanshugi (Anarchist-Communism)* (Tokyo, 1981) p. 336.
5. 'Hyaku Gojū Nen mae no Museifushugisha Andō Shōeki' ('Andō Shōeki: An Anarchist of 150 Years Ago') *Nihon Heimin Shinbun (Japan Common People's Newspaper)* 20 January 1908, p. 15.
6. Le Libertaire Group (eds.) *A Short History of the Anarchist Movement in Japan* (Tokyo, 1979) p. 3.
7. John Crump, *The Origins of Socialist Thought in Japan* (London, 1983) p. 277.
8. *Ōsugi Sakae Zenshū (Collected Works of Ōsugi Sakae)* (Tokyo, 1964) additional volume, p. 84.
9. *Arahata Kanson Chosaku Shū (Collected Works of Arahata Kanson)* (Tokyo, 1976) Vol. 2, p. 15.
10. Hagiwara Shintarō, *Nihon Anakizumu Rōdō Undō Shi (History of the Anarchist Labour Movement in Japan)* (Tokyo, 1969) pp. 101, 145.
11. Komatsu Ryūji, *Zenkoku Rōdō Kumiai Jiyū Rengōkai Shoshi (A Brief History of the All-Japan Libertarian Federation of Labour Unions)* (Tokyo, 1971) p. 98.
12. Peter Kropotkin, *The Conquest of Bread* (New York, 1972) p. 163.
13. *Ibid.*, p. 92 ('Commodities' has been changed to 'things' in line with the French original).
14. *Ibid.*, pp. 164, 104,
15. *Ibid.*, pp. 141-4.
16. P. A. Kropotkin, *Mutual Aid* (London, 1915) p. 11.
17. Daidōji Saburō, 'Makareta Tane wa Me o Fuite' ('Scattered Seeds Send Forth Shoots') in Ōshima (1981) p. 314.
18. Saitō Masahiro in Ōshima (1981) p. 309.
19. For Kropotkin's attitude towards syndicalism, see Martin A. Miller, *Kropotkin* (Chicago, 1976) pp. 176-7 and Alain Pengam, 'Anarcho-Communism' in Maximilien Rubel and John Crump (eds.) *Non-Market Socialism in the 19th and 20th Centuries* (London, 1987) pp. 74-6.
20. Hatta Shūzō, *Sanjikarizumu no Kentō* in Ōshima Seizaburō (ed.) *Museifukyōsanshugi (Anarchist-Communism)* (Tokyo, 1983) p. 8.
21. Hatta Shūzō, 'Sanjikarizumu ni tai suru Ichi Kōsatsu' ('An Enquiry into Syndicalism') in Ōshima (1983) p. 31.
22. *Ibid.*, p. 32.
23. See, for example, Hatta Shūzō, 'Jiyū Sobietto to Jiyū Kommyūn' ('Free Soviet and Free Commune') in Ōshima (1981) pp. 49-53.
24. Miller (1976) pp. 211-13, 241.
25. Ōshima (1981) p. 52.
26. Ōshima (1983) p. 15.

27. Hatta Shūzō, 'Sobietoshugisha o Hōmure' ('Bury the Sovietists') in Ōshima (1981) p. 167.
28. Ōshima (1983) p. 27.
29. *Ibid.*, p. 29.
30. Miller, pp. 190-1.
31. Ōshima (1981) p. 167.
32. Hatta Shūzō, 'Bakunin no Hen'ei' ('A Sketch of Bakunin') in Ōshima (1981) p. 156.
33. Ōshima (1983) p. 13.
34. *Ibid.*, p. 9.
35. Karl Marx, *Selected Works* (London, 1942) Vol. 2, pp. 563-5.
36. Kropotkin (1972) pp. 175-89.
37. Ōshima (1981) p. 166.
38. Hatta Shūzō, 'Shitagauredo Hishō Suru Jinrui no Rekishi' ('The Soaring Trajectory of Human History') in Ōshima (1981) p. 4.
39. *Ibid.*, pp. 6-7.
40. Ōshima (1983) p. 14.
41. *Ibid.*
42. Hatta Shūzō, 'Warera no Keizaigaku o Juritsu Seyo' ('Let's Establish Our Own Economics') in Ōshima (1981) p. 116.
43. Ōshima (1983) p. 33.
44. Ōshima (1981) p. 59.
45. *Ibid.*, p. 60.
46. *Ibid.*, p. 52.
47. Hatta Shūzō, 'Rōnō Kokka to Nōkō Jiyū Shi' ('The Workers' and Peasants' State and the Peasants' and Artisans' Free City') in Ōshima (1981) p. 153.
48. *Ibid.*
49. Rubel and Crump (1987) p. 79.

The Strategic Significance of the 1911 Anglo-Japanese Alliance

VALDO FERRETTI

On 5 April 1910 the Japanese government stressed in an official document that the Anglo-Japanese alliance was the 'marrow' of imperial foreign policy[1] and it is worth noting that it was drawn up at a critical moment in the history of the alliance. Thorough study has been devoted to the evolution of the alliance and the conclusions arrived at probably do not require revision as far as the course of the diplomatic negotiations and the domestic roots of British foreign policy are concerned. On Japan's side, however, renewal of the alliance in 1911 is still a subject of debate.

On the eve of the birth of the alliance in 1902, Japan and Great Britain had intended to persuade Russia to withdraw its troops stationed in Manchuria following the Boxer Rising and to halt its advance in China. This aim was maintained at the time of the first renewal in 1905, during the Russo-Japanese war, but much of its effectiveness diminished in 1907 since the agreements on Central Asia between London and St Petersburg on the one hand, and between Tokyo and the Tsar's empire, on the other hand, brought detente among the three powers.[2] Between 1905 and 1911 the character of the alliance was modified by various circumstances such as the change in government in England, developing antagonism between Japan and China, the nature of British policy in East Asia, and the attitudes of public opinion in Britain and in the Empire.[3] By 1911, when the alliance was renewed five years before its expiry, so many features of the international environment had changed from a decade before that the repercussions on the strategic significance of the alliance merit reassessment. The years between 1906 and 1910 were accompanied by worsening relations between Japan and the United States, particularly after the Taft administration assumed office in 1909 and proposed to internationalise the railway system in Manchuria.[4] The result was improved understanding between Tokyo and St Petersburg: each shared similar views concerning the Open Door policy in China and took a common stand against the American move.

The most striking aspect of the Anglo-Japanese treaty, signed on 13 July 1911, was the proviso that if one of the two contracting parties should conclude a general arbitration treaty with another power, the former would not be obliged to extend military assistance to its partner in the alliance in the contingency of war between the latter and any other signatory of the arbitration treaty. Since the negotiations resulted from a British proposal to modify the alliance in the light of a general arbitration treaty being signed, certain historians, following some of the Japanese newspapers of the period and speeches made by opposition politicians, have concluded that through renewal, Britain resolved to deny support to Japan in the event of war between Japan and the United States.[5] For the same reason the United States should not be seen as the hypothetical enemy against which the treaty was conceived. Some scholars believe that Russia fulfilled that role but such a view is difficult to support. Already in 1907 the *genro* and resident-general in Korea, Ito Hirobumi, had emphasised that the alliance had become less important because of improving relations with Russia. His more influential colleague, Yamagata Aritomo, continued to view favourably cooperation with Russia and in 1910 the two governments signed a political *entente*.[6] By 1907 the Japanese army, too, seems to have decided that, in the event of war with Russia, the alliance with Great Britain would become of little value.[7] American enthusiasm for arbitration agreements was inspired by pacifist notions and by the conviction of President Taft that judicial methods of solving international controversies should be pursued. Hence the United States developed similar initiatives with France and Germany also.[8] Moreover, it has been argued that Japan still feared a clash with Russia in 1911 in spite of the *ententes* of 1907 and 1910. The Japanese army asked for two divisions to be sent to the continent and a rumour reached Tokyo that the Russian finance minister was planning an anti-Japanese combination with America, just as critical problems concerning the Chinese-Korean border were taking shape.[9] Russia's attitude towards Mongolia and North China also caused suspicion and mistrust.[10]

Strong counter-arguments can be advanced against this view. The Japanese army exaggerated dangers on the continent in order to face the navy's competition for allocation of the defence budget, which could be cut by the cabinet.[11] The possibility of an American-Russian combination vanished when the Manchurian railway question exploded.[12] Suspicion in a strictly diplomatic sense continued to be felt but during the Chinese revolution in 1911 and 1912 both the Foreign Ministry and *genro* Yamagata preferred to keep close to Russia and the problems and misunderstandings which arose were solved easily through diplomatic channels.[13]

The above considerations do not suggest in any way that America was the new or principal enemy contemplated by the Anglo-Japanese alliance. The national defence plan approved in 1907 did not include the hypothesis that Britain would fight with Japan in a conflict with the United States and the foreign minister, Komura Jutaro, pointed out on 17 November 1910, that in spite of any legal commitment, Britain would not, in his view, help Japan militarily in that case. It could be said that the Japanese allowed the alliance to be changed because its new form did not connote anything substantially new, and in fact they did not try seriously to resist the British wish to insert the clause on arbitration. A further speculation is that even before negotiations began in September 1910, the significance attached by Tokyo to the treaty did not basically concern a possible war with America or Russia. Two explanations of this aspect have been advanced. According to one what Japan really wanted was an ally on whom to count amidst delicate and complex Chinese matters, and, for this reason - political rather than military - the pact with London kept its weight.[14] An alternative interpretation is that Japan was fearful of Germany and the Anglo-Japanese alliance was adapting itself to the state of European politics and especially to the Anglo-German naval race.

Against this view, too, solid counter-arguments have been put forward. According to these there is not enough evidence[15] that England attached anti-German meaning to the treaty with Japan, even if it assisted in concentrating warships in the North Sea by withdrawing them from the Far East, where Japan was expected to guard British interests. Furthermore, it is not clear why Japan should fear conflict with Germany, which did maintain a strong far-eastern squadron but lacked a chain of naval bases for the transfer of a large fleet from Europe.[16] For this reason even strict Anglo-French neutrality would have probably doomed the *Reich* to failure in case of war with Japan. Therefore, we may assume that Germany constituted a slight threat to Japan. To sum up, an authoritative study published more than fifteen years ago observed that assessment was rendered difficult because the evidence was too thin to grapple with the minds of Japanese leaders,[17] and rightly stressed that diplomatic sources alone were of insufficient help in solving the problem.

I shall examine this matter again by utilising a few Japanese documents which have been made available in recent years. To these will be added previously known sources.

As stated above, negotiations were generally amicable and the Japanese did not intend to press opposition to British proposals. Only less than one month before final signature was an attempt made to limit change. The Japanese Foreign Ministry tried to obtain a text for article 5 reading: 'it is agreed that nothing in this Agreement shall entail upon such Contracting Party an obligation to go to war with the Power with whom such Treaty of Arbitration is in force unless such third Power joins or is joined by one or more powers in war against the other Contracting Party.'[18] On 30 June, following conversations in London, the Japanese government dropped the last clause but Komura proposed an exchange of carefully worded memoranda which basically kept the same meaning with some additions. One is worth noting as it reads: 'in case a third power, not having in force a treaty of General Arbitration with one of the allies, should contemplate joining with a power having in force such a treaty in war against the other Ally, it would be incumbent on the Ally having such treaty, to exhaust its best efforts, to the extent of using its naval forces, to prevent such contemplated coalition.'[19]

These documents show that Komura envisaged a foreseeable hostile coalition to which a country bound to Britain by arbitral agreement could take part. Even though his proposals were rejected by London, the episode allows us to understand that the Japanese cabinet was probably worried by the naval strength of the supposed coalition while the desire to obtain a written guarantee by Britain leads us to appreciate that the danger was felt to be real. This tentative conclusion is supported by fresh evidence. In 1980 the diary of Takarabe Takeshi, at that time

Vice-Minister of the Japanese navy, was opened to scholars in the National Diet Library in Tokyo and proved to be of considerable importance for late Meiji political history even before its partial publication. This source includes two entries dealing with the third Anglo-Japanese alliance. On 1 July Takarabe says[20] he had visited the navy minister, Saito Makoto, who belonged to the same Satsuma faction as he did, and that he had been shown the text of the treaty approved the day before by the cabinet.[21] They discussed it and Saito added that the government had decided to renounce the above considered proviso included in the draft of article 5. Takarabe concluded: 'I think that it was a great pity. I said it promptly to the Minister himself.' The diary tells us also that the renewal of the alliance was examined on 15 July in a meeting of high navy officers to which, among others, Takarabe himself and the chief of the general staff, Ijuin Goro, participated, just after the treaty had been signed and ratified. They had to discuss publication of the text but the chief of the education bureau, Sakamoto Toshiazu, commented that a step had been taken which would deprive the Anglo-Japanese alliance of all of its value in future.[22] In other words this source confirms that strategic concern for the change in the alliance was connected with naval matters, and in this way sheds light on the expression 'to the extent of using its naval forces,' used in the memorandum. Moreover, it suggests that the contingency of fighting without the British umbrella was worrying the vice-minister and other navy men.

But what circumstances did they have in mind? There is no direct answer. In no way did confidence in Britain appear to have been lost. Later in 1911, in the early stages of the Chinese revolution, the chief of the military affairs bureau, Tochiuchi Kaijiro, on 15 November 1911,[23] drafted a further memorandum on the attitude of each foreign power interested in China, arguing that while America was expected to antagonise Japan, Britain's cooperation had to be cultivated in order to check Washington. It is reasonable to deduce, therefore, that a few months earlier, Britain was not expected to join Japan's possible foes. Thus in instructing the Japanese ambassador in London to hand over the June memorandum to the Foreign Office, Komura had explained that the British must be told that Japan had to anticipate a situation in which Britain might conclude general arbitration treaties with countries other than the United States.[24] This could be interpreted as diplomatic astuteness but the problem of hypothetical enemies other than America appears to be be occurring again.

We have seen through *Takarabe Nikki* how the navy reacted but it is now clear that in the national defence plan of 1907, America was only regarded as a fictitious enemy with which no concrete likelihood of conflict was being considered. The admirals looked to friendly relations with the United States and Britain at the time when they feared that the new German fleet could be used in East Asia. They foresaw that because of events in Europe, a war between the German *Reich* and the British Empire could occur, in which Japan would have to fulfil its duties under the Anglo-Japanese alliance.[25] Interestingly, the danger that Germany could secure new bases outside Europe and in the respective spheres of influence was a common fear in both the American and Japanese navies.[26] Between 1906 and 1911 the real hypothetical foe seemed to be China, which was attempting to recover its national rights under the last Ch'ing emperor and was too weak to challenge Japan but might become dangerous if supported by other powers interested in restraining Japan's influence on the continent. One is led to believe that any concrete threat of war should have come from China and that by 1911 both America and Germany, but especially the latter, could be seen as the fulcrum of an anti-Japanese coalition. In 1907 and 1908 diplomatic exchanges had taken place between these three powers and on the eve of the Manchurian railways question in 1909, both China and Germany had sided with the USA. After the end of this crisis, Germany and the United States were identified as the source of support China would seek in order to frustrate Japan.[27] Therefore it is logical to state that in 1911 the Japanese cabinet, including the navy and Foreign Ministry, saw the alliance with Britain as a tool against that kind of coalition.

In my view there is some evidence to confirm this speculation. It is well known that, following an initiative of the resident-general in Korea, Ito Hirobumi, a general inquiry on the functioning of Japanese foreign policy had been promoted in the second half of 1907. Katsura Taro, a past and future prime minister, was aware of Ito's anxiety and the foreign minister, Hayashi Tadasu, reported its results to the *genro* and to the cabinet. Among the powers the most alarming for Ito was Germany whose activity in China, naval policy, and attitude to Russia led to fear that anti-Japanese feelings could be fostered in China.[28] Hayashi considered the Kaiser's empire to be much weaker in the Far East than in Europe and realised that after the Algeciras conference of 1906 even there it was isolated. He noted that the Kaiser's view of Japan was not benevolent but stressed that no conflict existed in commercial matters. In his report he ended the paragraph touching on the *Reich* with the following revealing words: 'Maintaining from the very start that Germany does not need to carry on some intriguing for the purpose of changing the balance of power in the Far East, we should in my opinion make more and more solid the Anglo-Japanese alliance in order to face such a chance.'[29] This document, dated 29 November 1907, had come immediately after the treaties made by Japan with France and Russia, and the Kaiser's proposals to Washington. We know that they were largely inspired by European developments and by the wish to break the system built by Japan by linking itself to the Franco-Russian group and to Britain.[30] Consequently, it can be understood that Anglo-German rivalry led Tokyo to take account of Germany as a possible enemy just when Japan's rapprochement to Paris and St Petersburg enticed Germany to counter Japan in China; and in such a contest, the Anglo-Japanese alliance itself started to assume an anti-German direction. Hence it continued to assist Japan's strategy even while becoming less helpful vis-à-vis Russia or the United States.

This seems to indicate deeper reasons for Japan's entrance into the

First World War. Concern for Germany was strong in the Foreign Ministry and in the navy. A recent study has emphasised that the clique which took over power in *Kaigunsho* after the fall of the Yamamoto cabinet in 1914 was upset by German strength in China and the western Pacific. Probably for this reason it welcomed the declaration of war on Germany in August 1914, which in turn was legally founded in the Anglo-Japanese alliance.[31] Apart from the personal feelings of the foreign minister, Kato Takaaki, and of the old prime minister, Okuma Shigenobu, a continuous range of evidence shows that, as the backbone of imperial foreign policy, the alliance linked Japan's choices to the transformation of the balance of power in Europe, by leading them to take account of developments both there and in China. Hence the decision for war in 1914 can be seen as a natural outcome of all these premises. It offers additional evidence that Chinese considerations alone should be seen as having limited impact in the context of Japanese diplomacy after the Russo-Japanese war.

NOTES

1. *Nihon Gaikō Monjō* (thereafter NGB), Vol. 43/1, doc. n. 13.
2. See the classical study of E. W. Edwards, 'The Far Eastern Agreements' of 1907', *Journal of Modern History*, 1954. N. 4, pp. 340-55.
3. Cf. specially I. Nish, *Alliance in Decline. A Study in Anglo-Japanese Relations 1908-23*, London, 1972, and P. Lowe, *Great Britain and Japan, 1911-15: A Study of British Far Eastern Policy* London, 1969.
4. W. V. Scholes and M. V. Scholes, *The Foreign Policies of the Taft Administration*, Columbia (Missouri), 1970, pp. 10-1 (fn.), 109ff.
5. P. Renouvin, *Le Problème d'Extrème Orient*, Paris, 1946, pp. 239-40. A Iriye, *Pacific Estrangement, Japanese and American Expansion 1897-1911*, Cambridge, Mass., 1972, pp. 228-9. Cf. A. Dennis, *The Anglo-Japanese Alliance*, Berkeley, 1966, pp. 37-8.
6. Itō Takashi and G. Akita, *Yamagata Aritomo to 'Jinshū Kyōsō ron,'* 'Kindai Nihon Kenkyū,' 1985, pp. 95-118, sp. p. 104. Tanaka Naokichi, *Nichi-Rō Kyōshō Ron*, in Ueda Toshio (ed.), *Kamikawa Sensei Kanreki Kinen. Kindai Nihon Gaikoshi no Kenkyū*, Tokyo, 1956, sp. p. 313 ff. Several documents in NGB, Vol 40/1, cf. Oyama Azusa, Yamagata Aritomo *Teikoku Kokubō Hōshin An*, 'Kokusai Seiji,' 1960/3, pp. 170-7.
7. Kitaoka Shinichi, *Nihon Rikugun to Tairiku Seisaku*, Tokyo, 1985, (2nd ed.), p. 16.
8. *British Documents on the Origins of the War* (BD), Vol VIII, p. 542 (fn.). *Die Grosse Politik der Europaeischen Kabinette 1870-1917* (GP), Vol 32, p. 227 (fn.).
9. A. Dennis, op. cit., pp. 32-3; Moriyama Shigenori *Nicchō Heigō no Kokusai Kankei-Chōsen Mondai to Manshū Mondai no Renkan*, 'Kindai Nihon Kenkyu, 1985, pp. 69-94, sp. p. 88ff.; Kitaoka, op. cit., pp. 67-8.
10. Ikei Masaru (ed.), Uchida Kōsai, Tokyo, 1969, pp. 202ff.
11. See for instance Banno Junji, *Taishō Seihen. 1900 Nen Taisei no Hōkai*, Kyoto, 1982, 97ff.
12. Moriyama, op. cit., p. 91.
13. See, for instance, Nakami Tatsuo, *A Protest against the Concept of the 'Middle' Kingdom: The Mongols and the 1911 Revolution*, in Etō Shinkichi and H. Z. Schiffrin (eds.) *The 1911 Revolution in China*, Tokyo, 1984, pp. 129-49.
14. Murajima Shigeru, *Daisanji Nichi-Ei Dōmei no Seikaku to Igi*, 'Kokusai Seiji,' 1971/1, pp. 75-92, Cf. Shimanuki Takeji, *Nichi-Rō Sensō igō ni Okeru Kokubō Hōshin, Jōyō Heiryoku, Yōhei Yoryo no Hensen*, 'Gunji Shigaku,' 1973, N. 32, pp. 2-14.
15. I. Nish, op. cit., p. 71.
16. Nomura Ōtojiro *Nihon Gaikō Seijishi no Kenkyū*, Tokyo, 1982, pp. 7-8.
17. I. Nish, op. cit., p. 73.
18. NGB, Vol. 44, doc. n. 94.
19. NGB, Vol. 44, doc. n. 98. *Betsuden*.
20. Banno Junji, Hirose Yasuaki, Masuda Tomoko, Watanabe Yasuo (eds.), *Takarabe Takeshi Nikki. Kaigun Shikan Jidai*, Vol. 1, Tokyo, 1983, pp. 232-3.

21. As confirmed in *Kokkai Toshōkan, Kensei Shiryōshitsu, Saitō Makoto Monjō, Nikki*, Vol. 44, entry of June 30th. Komura's instructions relating to the above discussed *memorandum* were sent on 30/6/1911 also, but most probably after the meeting of the Cabinet, held at 9 p.m. Thus the Foreign Ministry concern for the British guarantee seems to have been similar to that of Takarabe.

22. *Takarabe Takeshi Nikki*, cit., p. 236.

23. Hatano Masaru, *Shingai Kakumei to Nihon Kaigun no Taiō*, 'Gunji Shigaku' 1986, 21/4 especially pp. 20-1.

24. NGB, Vol. 44, doc. n. 98, cit. p. 369.

25. Shimanuki Takeji, cit., sp. p. 4-5; Hatano Sumio and Kondō Shinji (eds.), *Shimpojiumu Nichro Senso*, 'Gunji Shigaku,' 1981, 16/4, pp. 15-30, sp. p. 19ff. Masuda Tomoko, *Kaigun Kakuchō Mondai no Seiji Katei, 1906-14*, 'Kindai Nihon Kenkyū,' 1982, pp. 411-33. *Senshi Sōshō (Nomura Minoru), Daihonei Kaigunbu Rengō Kantai (1) Kaisen Made*, Tokyo, 1975, pp. 103-7, which directly refers to Satō's Tetsutarō's *Teikoku Kokubō Shiron* (rep. Tokyo, 1979).

26. See J. H. Maurer, *American Naval Concentration and the German Battle Fleet*, 'Journal of Strategic Studies,' 1983/3, n. 2, pp. 147-181, sp. pp. 155-9.

27. Tanaka Naokichi, op. cit., pp. 328-9. Eaba Akira, *Nichirō Sensō go no Tairiku Seisaku*, 'Kokusai seiji,' 1960/3, pp. 134-150 [rep. in Kurihara Ken (ed.), *Taimammō Seisakushi no Ichimen*, Tokyo, 1981, pp. 62-86].

28. NGB, Vol. 40/3, doc. n. 2199.

29. NGB, Vol. 40/3, doc. n. 2200, p. 797.

30. Since the old article of L. J. Hall, *The Abortive German-American-Chinese Entente of 1907-8*, 'Journal of Modern History,' 1929, Vol. 1, n. 2, pp. 177-235.

31. Hirama Yōichi, *Daichiji Seikai Daisen e no Sanka to Kaigun Sansen Ishi Kettei o Megutte*, 'Gunji Shigaku,' 22/1, 1986, pp. 27-37.

Emperorship as a National Symbol in Taishō Japan (1912-1926)

OLAVI K. FÄLT

The Meiji Era in the history of Japan began with the Japanese emulating the modernisation process in the West. For this end the ruling oligarchy strived to raise the Emperor into a symbol of national unity and loyalty. The actual cornerstone on which the Emperor's position as a symbol rested was the assumption that the imperial family was of a divine nature having descended from Amaterasu Ōmikami, the Sun Goddess, the literary tradition of whom goes back at least to the historical scripts of the eighth century. This notion had subsequently been taken a step further by Kitabatake Chakafusa, a fourteenth-century historian and politician. In his book *Jinnō Shōtōki* (On The Legitimacy Of The Imperial Line) he put emphasis on the divine nature of the imperial family and on the special relationship between the Emperor and his nation, for which he used the term '*kokutai*', or national entity. This term came later to include all the characteristics and ideals the Japanese regarded as particular to them. Imperial mysticism was still a living part of the Japanese cultural heritage even at the beginning of the twentieth century.[1]

The Emperor's position was officially defined in the 1889 Constitution. The definition was based on Lorenz von Stein's idea of a social monarchy that would reconcile the competing interests of various social groups. The Emperor would personify public will, while at the same time he would stand above class struggles, defend the weak against the strong, and safeguard social harmony. In the Japanese interpretation the emphasis on harmony, which was well in keeping with Japanese traditions, was highlighted, while the social side took second place. According to the Meiji Constitution the Government was answerable to the Emperor, whose rights included declaring war, signing treaties and functioning as the commander-in-chief of the armed forces. The real influence of the Diet (parliament) was limited to accepting or rejecting the budget, i.e., it possessed the authority to veto taxes.[2] All in all, the Meiji Constitution was Emperor-centric to a large extent.

The purpose of this paper is to study the kind of national image and national endeavours *The Japan Times* and the *Osaka Mainichi* reflect in their articles concerning the Emperor and the Emperorship, as well as to find out what connotations were associated with the Emperor as a symbol.

The analyses are made at junctures at which the Emperor, the Emperorship and the Empire were in the focus of particular public attention, to wit, the Emperor's birthday celebrations (*Tenchōsetsu*), the celebration of the mythical founding of Japan (Kigensetsu, 11.2.660 B.C.), the Crown Prince Hirohito's European tour in 1921, his wedding in 1924 and the death of Emperor Yoshihito in 1926.

National interests had been present at the founding of *The Japan Times*, giving some justification to the idea that the paper was Japan's unofficial mouthpiece directed towards foreign readers. Leading Japanese statesmen had come to realise in the 1890s that there was a need to establish a Japanese-owned English-language newspaper in Japan, reporting on news events in Japan and the Far East. Their main interest, however, was publicising Japanese views in English. The men to take the decisive step were Fukuzawa Yukichi, the renowned founder of the Keiō University and an advocate of western culture, and Itō Hirobumi, probably the most eminent Japanese statesman of his time. According to Itō Japan needed an English-language newspaper that would support the government and interpret its policies to the outside world. He persuaded his secretary, Mr Zumota Motosada, who had already expressed a keen interest in the matter, along with Mr Yamada Suehara to found the newspaper. They received financial support from such sources as Mitsui, Mitsubishi, the Bank of Japan and Nippon Yusen Kaisha. The first issue rolled off the printing press on 22 March 1897. After the ownership of the newspaper passed to the Japanese news office Kokusai Tsushisha in 1914, several management changes took place, until in 1921 the Ministry of Foreign Affairs and the Mitsui Chamber of Commerce began to give financial support to the newspaper.[3]

The first issue of the *Osaka Mainichi* was published on 12 April 1922, the idea being that the English language newspaper would be a copy of the original Japanese paper, the *Osaka Mainichi Shimbun*, which had a circulation of over one million. There was one limiting factor though: the size of the newspaper was restricted to four pages only. The man behind the project was the president of the newspaper publishing house, Mr Motoyama Hikoichi, who nurtured the idea of creating an independent Japanese-owned English language newspaper that would act as a counterweight to three other English-language papers. The objection to these latter was that *The Japan Advertiser* and *The Japan Chronicle* were owned by foreign publishers, and *The Japan Times* was regarded as the mouthpiece of the Ministry of Foreign Affairs.[4]

A new Emperor on the throne signified something over and above its immediate meaning: the dawn of a new era with high hopes of an even brighter future. The Meiji Era drew to its close with the death of the highly respected Emperor Mutsuhito in 1912. The monarch of the new Taishō Era was Emperor Yoshihito, and from the very beginning of his reign it was hoped that he would begin a process of democratisation.

The Japan Times regarded the new Emperor's initial acts as tell-tale signals indicative of a ruler who had his nation's best interests at heart. These undertakings included granting a handful of high-ranking officials permission to pay their last respects to the deceased Emperor in a chamber formerly accessible only to members of the royal family, and redirecting the imperial route from the Ayoma palace to the court so as to cause the least possible disturbance to public traffic en route. These actions were considered the harbinger of a new democratic era:

> To put it in a nutshell, the indications of the new reign are for the growth of a democratic tendency.[5]

The Japan Times saw democracy as the leading ideology of the new era, and looked upon it as the real foundation of true righteousness (the very name of the dawning era, Taishō, stood for Great Righteousness), which is why the paper considered it a felicitous circumstance indeed that the era had begun under such unforeseen signs:

> ...we hail with deep thankfulness that the beginning of the new era of Taishō (Great Righteousness) is marked with indications of a growing democratic tendency.

The newspaper stated that the era of the late Emperor Mutsuhito had not offered favourable conditions for this kind of thinking for the Emperor had been born and educated in the spirit of an altogether different age.[7]

In spite of the fact that the Meiji Era was so highly praised, the reference to a new era of democracy and to the Meiji Emperor's background revealed that there was a certain measure of discontent in the way the newspaper looked upon the era of the previous Emperor, despite the rapid development that had taken place in Japan during his reign. At the funeral of the Meiji Emperor, *The Japan Times* noted that although a lot of progress had been made during the preceding era, the new Emperor faced a full workload before Japan could claim to have reached the level of the world's most developed nations. The newspaper was particularly keen to impress upon its readers that they should renounce the notion of the moral culture of the East being on a par with that of the West. Unless this misconception was expelled, the Taishō Era would not become the long-awaited period of moral and ethical development. *The Japan Times* believed that had the late Emperor lived longer, he would have taken steps towards abolishing the aforementioned fallacy.[8] The paper's intention was obviously to make an appeal to the new Emperor.

In order to promote democracy, which *The Japan Times* held as the leading ideology of the age, the paper consoled those fearing that the democratisation of the royal court would diminish its holiness, with the thought that in return there would be a closer relationship between the royal house and the people: 'If the new Emperor will not be a demigod, he will be a beloved head of the State.'[9] The paper considered it essential that the future development of Japan be based on western democratic and moral ideas:

> The Japanese nation is fully conscious that all the reform work was not completed with the Meiji era, and is determined to carry under the leadership of the new Emperor those intellectual and spiritual reforms which are necessary to make Japan a modern nation in the highest sense of the term.'[10]

While the Meiji era was interpreted as the age of material and organisational reforms, it was assumed that that of the new Emperor - raised in a totally new environment - would become one of moral and mental modernisation, presumably in the spirit of the early reforms in the reign of the Meiji Emperor.[11]

In addition to promoting democracy, *The Japan Times* deemed it important to establish international contacts with the western powers on an equal footing. The best way to reach that end was to reduce racial prejudice against the Japanese by improving the general living standard of the country.[12]

During the first years of Emperor Yoshihito's rule *The Japan Times* paid no special attention to days of national importance, often a mere mention of the official ceremonies sufficed.[13] However, the First World War, in which Japan joined the anti-German front, aroused patriotic sentiments, or rather forced such sentiments to be aroused owing to Japan's geographically restricted and relatively insignificant role in the actual war. This new patriotism was very much in evidence in the amount of attention the paper gave to the Emperor's birthday in 1915, displaying a substantial increase from previous years. References were made to the declaration of war on Germany, issued in the previous year, and to the feelings of darkness and gloom generated by it. Inferences can be drawn on the one hand concerning Japan's involvement in the war and on the other concerning the peaceful nature of the situation, indicating the nominal role Japan played in the warring events: '...in peace and glory in spite of the war the Emperor, to-day, celebrates the 36th anniversary of his birthday....'[14] The 1916 Kigensetsu also attracted unforeseen attention, though the cause may more likely be attributed to the fact that this was the first Kigensetsu after the new Emperor had officially taken the crown (in November 1915), than to the surge of patriotic emotions occasioned by the war.[15]

The increasing publicity afforded to these nationally important events during the war was a reflection of the anxiety generated by the war, although the expressed content of the articles amounted to little more than mere wishes of peace and success.[16] They did, nevertheless, draw attention to eminent national symbols.[17] This observation is further strengthened by the fact that there was a considerable decrease in the interest the paper exhibited towards these symbols after the war.[18]

However, the 1921 celebration of the 2580th anniversary of the mythical founding of Japan did receive ample attention. The actual starting off point that *The Japan Times* chose to employ in its presentation did not emerge from the obscurity of the past: they built the story around a Kigensetsu poem penned by Mrs Burnett, wife of an American military attaché. The poem, the paper felt, expressed a sympathetic interpretation of Japanese thinking.[19]

This choice was well in keeping with contemporary Japanese foreign policy with its emphasis on Anglo-Saxon cooperation. Needless to say, it was also well aligned with the realisation of the idea of international cooperation which was gaining momentum at the beginning of the Taishō Era. The choice was also an outsider's encouragement for the

Japanese to acknowledge the importance of their historical past and the values connected with it. Japan was at that very moment on the receiving end of a cultural attack from the West spearheaded by sports, cafes and democratic ideals.

The background for Japan's national ambition was traced back to the founding of the Empire, and the Rising Sun was perceived as the symbol of truth and development that had shone on the Empire and led the nation towards enlightenment.[20] Nevertheless, the epithets and aims that *The Japan Times* employed as the vehicle of expression (namely the great ideas of the Enlightenment: truth, progress and enlightenment) bear witness to a strong ideological preference for western cultural values.

An event that stirred the national consciousness even more than the 2580th anniversary of the Empire was the return of the Crown Prince Hirohito from an almost six-month-long European tour in September that year.[21] The tour was unique in many respects, but most of all because it was the first time that a member of the imperial family, the future Emperor, had travelled outside Japan.

The prince's triumphant welcome home epitomised the way he was seen as the nation's source of life and energy, and, above all, as the symbol of international cooperation: '…along the royal road to a better understanding with other nations of the world, to peace on earth and to goodwill towards all men.'[22] His trip was perceived as a sign of a new, more intimate system of international relationships based on a closer understanding between the East and the West. In its enthusiasm for the Prince the paper went as far as to consider his trip as having eradicated 'the semi-divine attributes associated with Emperors and Kings, not at all peculiar only to Japan…'[23] as well as having reinforced the people's ties of affiliation and loyalty towards him.[24] His tour was not only a victory for Japan, it was also a personal victory: '…he went; he saw; he conquered.'[25]

The policy of international understanding and cooperation that Japan had adopted at the beginning of the 1920s reached its culmination point in the Washington Conference in 1921-22. Among other things the conference agreed to restrict the size of the superpowers' navies; it replaced the Anglo-Japanese Alliance with the Pacific Treaty signed by the United States, Great Britain, France and Japan; and it attempted to secure the inviolability of China, advocated by the USA, by signing the open door agreement of the nine powers.[26] At the same time, the quest for the political basis in the national symbols found its zenith in a remark made by the General-Governor of Korea, Baron Saito, who was quoted, in the context of the Kigensetsu celebrations of 1922, as saying that patriotic pride that Japan had since time immemorial strived towards world peace:

> The doctrine of international goodwill and world peace which is written into the results of the Washington Conference has been the national doctrine of Japan since the founding of the Empire, more than twenty-five hundred years ago, six centuries before the birth of Christ.[27]

The nationalistic sentiments associated with the Crown Prince regained their topicality in January 1924 on the occasion of his wedding. The Prince's importance had grown because he had acted as regent after Emperor Yoshihito, his father, had been taken ill in the autumn of 1921. This added an extra dimension to the wedding; in one estimate the significance of the marriage had increased a thousand fold.[28]

The Japan Times already saw great promise in the Prince as the future Emperor, proclaiming that his European tour along with his subsequent spell as regent had created a strong confidence among his subjects in the future of the country.[29] In its actual congratulations the paper wished peace, advancement and enlightenment to his rule as regent and to his future rule as the Emperor.[30] In other words, the catchwords borrowed from the ideological world of the European Enlightenment reappeared once again.

In one private estimate the Prince was somewhat discordantly described as a saviour leading his nation towards democracy: 'Crown Prince, Democrat, Leader Destined to Save Japan.'[31] Though the evaluation failed to mention what the Prince was supposed to be saving his nation from, it did state that his ideal was to turn his country into a haven based on mutual love and respect; the sole claim the sovereign made to his people was obedience:

> All that is required on our part is to rally round him in one spirit
> and in faithful obedience to his call...[32]

Such a role, however, cannot readily be incorporated into the picture of the Crown Prince as a democratic ideal.

In another evaluation, written in the same vein, the national goal of Japan was not the adoption of western culture, nor was it the revival of Oriental civilisation, but the ideal was to be a nation standing on a foundation of justice and humanity. The Crown Prince was viewed as a leader who was rising to fulfil his divine and royal task.[33] Another similar opinion regarded Japan as the cradle of a new civilisation based on righteousness and peace, born from the finest heritage of western and Japanese cultures. It was hoped that the Prince would make Nippon a truly great nation.[34]

Democracy, although presented from an authoritarian point of view, righteousness and humanity seemed to be the most popular epithets associated either directly with the Crown Prince, or indirectly with the new Japan under him. On the one hand, these terms referred to the general international values of the 1920s: the outcome of the war was considered as the victory of democracy, and the realisation of righteousness and humanity as the goal of the League of Nations. On the other hand, these terms also connected with the idea of Japan occupying a special niche in the world, an idea with strong roots in traditional Japanese nationalism.

The pace of the Japanese pulse slackened in November 1926 when news came of Emperor Yoshihito's deteriorating health. The time had come again when people's minds turned to fundamental national values and symbols as the nation prayed for divine help for their ruler.[36]

The Emperor Yoshihito died on 25 December 1926. The event signified the end of an era and the beginning of a new one in the history of Japan.[37] The first comments offered by *The Japan Times* referred to the bygone era as the Glorious Era of Taishō, which could count among its accomplishments Japan's extended sphere of interest on the Asian continent, the continual increase in international cooperation, and the new parliamentary system of government, still on trial at that stage.[38]

The newspaper may have been assigning the idea of parliamentary government an extra emphasis when it concluded that the underlying causes for the late Emperor's illness may have been the pressures brought on by the idea of a novel parliamentary system and the shock of the Russian revolution. According to the paper, public opinion at the beginning of the Taishō Era expected the Crown to stay aloof of all matters political. Things had truly changed in comparison with the Meiji Era. British-style parliamentarism had gradually been introduced to Japan in such a way that the safety of the Crown seemed to depend on not interfering with politics. Not that the Emperor had been denied his right to rule, but rather that the subjects had grown accustomed to taking care of their own affairs instead of bothering the monarch with them. The transition period to parliamentarism and its accompanying political agitation, said *The Japan Times*, proved too heavy a burden for the young Emperor.[39]

In its editorial *The Japan Times* regarded the progress made during the Taishō Era, irrespective of its short duration, as being on a par with that of the Meiji Era. They pointed out the doubling of the gross national wealth, the advancement of scientific research in Japan and the country's conspicuous role in creating world peace. The paper concluded that the official term applied to the era, Great Righteousness, was particularly apt as it had constituted the aim of all governmental actions and policies. The paper wanted to make a special mention of Japan's involvement in the promotion of peace, which it said characterised the era in the same fashion as the build-up of military power had done the preceding Meiji Era.[40]

The evaluations of the situation published in *The Japan Times* are a clear indication that the paper supported peaceful international relationships and considered the emphasis put on military power and - as we have already noted - authoritarian rule as outdated ideas. The background for this attitude may be traced back to the already mentioned international atmosphere of the post First World War period with its emphasis on democracy and peaceful cooperation.

In spite of the strong weight put upon international cooperation, there was also a powerful Emperor-centric nationalism prevalent in Japan. The way *The Japan Times* saw it, Japan possessed something extraordinary, namely, the imperial institution, which was the polestar of its history and the uniting factor holding the nation together amid all turbulence:

> Under its benign influence all disintegrating elements are bound
> to crumble away; sectionalism and class war must give place to

national oneness and integrity... there will ever be unity of grief and indivisible fellowship in national anguish.[41]

In *The Japan Times'* opinion the history of Japan had been intimately intertwined with that of the imperial rule, so much so in fact that the two have at times been held practically identical. And although foreign critics had often presented the early history of the imperial institution as a legend, the faith the Japanese invested in it formed one of the most important pillars on which the life of the nation rested. The newspaper justified its claims by stating that because the early history was so difficult to verify, as it resided mainly in the minds of the people, the present would also shed light on the past:

We weave our present experience into a history, set it up as an ideal and allow ourselves to be guided by it.[42]

The Japan Times made a particular reference to the benevolence the Emperors had exhibited towards their subjects ever since the late Taishō Emperor.[43] No one could imitate the unique relationship between the ruler and the people. The Emperor might have an enormous authority but he had never used it to counter the best interests of his subjects.[44]

The new Emperor was from the outset connected with the goals once again associated with the new era, though the goals themselves had their origins in the previous era. As a person the Emperor was regarded as the image of his grandfather, the great Meiji Emperor, who founded modern Japan. With respect to his compassionate and sympathetic nature, he was also characterised as having taken after his mother.[45]

The name of the new era, Shōwa or Radiant Peace, provided a point of departure for the evaluation of the reign of the new Emperor. *The Japan Times*, in fact, deemed it very fitting to give such a name to the reign of the Emperor who had a profound interest in world peace. An arms race was less important than peaceful cooperation in the fields of culture and science:

We realise that the spirit of the times is not represented by the prevailing race in constructing cruisers, but by the peaceful and cultural undertakings of the League of Nations and by numerous international scientific congresses.[46]

The Japan Times put such a high premium on the change of eras that it presented a novel interpretation of the past from the point of view of the dawning era. From the old perspective the Meiji Era appeared as the time of material and organisational progress,[47] from the new one it was construed above all as the period of military advancement,[48] during which the country had fought a series of successful wars and attained a position in the front row of nations. The Taishō Era, for its part, had signified the end of Military Japan and the preparation for founding the Kingdom of God in international relationships. The Shōwa Era, in keeping with its name, would be the time of peaceful accomplishments and the time for fulfilling earlier promises.[49] It was hoped that the peace and goodwill that the new era seemed to hold would also extend to the internal affairs of Japan.[50]

In spite of the fact that the features emphasising the uniqueness of Japan were present at the death of Emperor Yoshihito, *The Japan Times* did not consider the closing Taishō Era as a period when strong patriotic overtones were attached to the position of the Emperor as a symbol. A fact that weighs in favour of this interpretation is that *The Osaka Mainichi* and the *Tokyo Nichi Nichi* were worried about the lack of reverence people displayed towards the Kigensetsu of 1926.[51] It is evident, though, that the moment of crisis, the Emperor's illness and his subsequent death, revealed the utmost priority meted out to the patriotic sentiments connected with the Emperor; but it is likewise evident that under the circumstances, under the compelling social pressure, the papers had no choice but to write what they did.

While the nation held its breath and followed the progress of the Emperor's illness, *The Osaka Mainichi* followed the example set by *The Japan Times* in stressing that the imperial family was the sole source of national virtues and qualities. As long as the loyalty invested in the Crown and the love towards Japan endured, the real spirit of the Yamato State (Japan) would live on for all eternity.[52]

Upon the death of the Emperor *The Osaka Mainichi* - in the wake of *The Japan Times* again - commented on the major role Japan had assumed in international affairs during his reign, and it did not forget to mention the development of democracy in the country either. As far as the latter issue was concerned, the paper thought that it was of supreme importance that the Imperial Oath sworn at the beginning of the Meiji Restoration, allowing public opinion to settle all matters, had finally come true as all male subjects got the vote. The Emperor received full credit:

> He has failed in nothing to fulfil the far-sighted policy of his Imperial father and has done everything for the glorious development of the Empire.[53]

In what was apparently an attempt to accentuate the significance of democracy, *The Osaka Mainichi* did not fall short of extolling such virtues of the late Emperor, as passivity, as meekness of heart, forbearance and benevolence, as well as his humble and unostentatious manner, which were, the paper concluded, very befitting characteristics for an Emperor of a new democratic era.[54]

The democratic disposition of the new Emperor, Hirohito, was also highly acclaimed,[55] along with his intelligence, courage and other virtues, which were known around the globe.[56]

The expectations concerning internal and external harmony that *The Osaka Mainichi* pinned on the new Shōwa Era matched those of *The Japan Times*. Japan had a mission: to promote mutual understanding between Japan and other nations in the spirit of the new era. The press had a meaningful role to play in this context by making Japan known outside the borders of the country, as well as in familiarising the Japanese public with other nations. *The Osaka Mainichi* was fully convinced that with the new Emperor at the helm, the nation would be able to steer the ship of state safely on the high seas of peace.[57]

While *The Osaka Mainichi* associated the Emperor with enhancing democracy, international cooperation, peace and harmony, it nevertheless conveyed a message in conflict with the democratic ideals that it advocated, namely an uncompromising loyalty to the Emperor in the construction of the prosperity and glory of the Empire:

> In the hour of our deep mourning over the demise of the late Emperor, we herewith vow to exert our utmost efforts to help the cause of prosperity and glory of the Empire, and thus prove in deed that we are not ungrateful children of the Throne, in whose benevolence we have our own being and existence.[58]

The basic problem of who was to determine the direction towards prosperity and glory, and what would be the precise content of these concepts remained unsolved. Loyalty to the Emperor did not necessarily involve international cooperation, peace or democracy, though they were certainly associated with the Emperor in that situation. Irrespective of the fact that these central ideas of western liberalism won favour in Japan during the Taishō Era, the fundamental contradiction between them and the demand for absolute obedience persisted. Both papers aspired to connect the Emperor with democracy and international cooperation. It was apparently their intent to promote them with the aid of the emperorship, but it was an endeavour which did not make it impossible to associate exactly opposite ideas with the highest spiritual and political authority in the land, the symbol of the Emperor.

NOTES

1. *Kojiki* (Translated with an Introduction and Notes by Donald L. Philippi, Tokyo, 1977; *Nihongi, Chronicles of Japan from the Earliest Times to A.D. 697* (Translated from the Original Chinese and Japanese by W. G. Aston, C. M. G. With an Introduction to the New Edition by Terence Barrow. Two Volumes in One, Tokyo, 1972); G. W. Robinson, *Early Japanese Chronicles; The Six National Histories* (Historians of China and Japan. Edited by W. G. Beasley and E. G. Pulleyblank. *Historical Writings on the People of Asia*, reprinted, London, 1965), pp. 215-222; Delmer M. Brown, *Nationalism in Japan. An Introductory Historical Analysis* (Berkeley and Los Angeles, 1955), passim; Herman Webb, *The Japanese Imperial Institution in the Tokugawa Period* (New York, 1968), passim; H. Paul Varley, *Imperial Restoration in Medieval Japan* (New York, 1971), passim; David Magarey Earl, *Emperor and Nation in Japan. Political Thinkers of the Tokugawa Period* (Seattle, 1964), passim; see also Olavi K. Fält, *Keisarius Japanin poliittisen ajattelun historiassa* (*The Emperorship in the history of Japanese political philosophy*) (Faravid IX, Jyväskylä, 1986), pp. 165-187; Olavi K. Fält, *Keisarin-kuva Japanissa kansallisen olemuksen ja pyrkimysten tulkkina Meiji-kauden lopulla* (Faravid X, Jyväskylä, 1987), pp. 249-257. On propagating Tenchōsetsun at the beginning of the Meiji Era, see Albert Altman, *The Emergence of the Press in Meiji Japan* (Princeton University, Ph.D., 1965), pp. 145-146.
2. W. G. Beasley, *The Modern History of Japan* (Third Revised Edition, First Tuttle Edition, Tokyo, 1982), pp. 130-131.
3. Shinichi Hasekawa, 'Rivalries Marked Early English-Language Journalism' (*The Japan Times*, 19 July 1982, 30000th Issue Commemorative Supplement (I); Ki Kimura, 'Pioneers in Paper's Past' (*The Japan Times*, 1 June 1956); Kokushi bunken kaisetsu zoku (Endō Motō, Shimomura Fujio hen, Tōkyō, 1965), p. 436; 'Times Celebrates Diamond Jubilee. Travels Long, Difficult Road since Foundation in 1897' (*The Japan Times*, 22 March 1957, Anniversary Supplement); Harry Emerson Wildes, *Social Currents in Japan. With Special Reference to the Press* (Chicago, 1927), pp. 289-291. The Japan Times in nimi 1918-1940 The Japan Times and Mail.
4. 'Highlights of Half a Century's History,' *Mainichi Daily News*, 12 April 1972; Shingero Takaishi, 'How the English Mainichi was Started' (*The Mainichi*, 12 April 1957); Wildes, pp. 275-278. *The Osaka Mainichi* nimi 1925-1940 The Osaka Mainichi and the Tokyo Nichinichi.
5. 'Our New Sovereign,' *The Japan Times*, 9 August 1912. See Fält, Keisarin-kuva, pp. 255-256.
6. *Ibid.*
7. *Ibid.*
8. 'The State Funeral,' *The Japan Times*, 13 September 1912.
9. 'The Spiritual Problem of Taisho Era,' *The Japan Times*, 19 September 1912.

10. *Ibid.*
11. See 'An Inspiring Anniversary,' *The Japan Times*, 30 July 1913.
12. *Ibid.*
13. See *The Japan Times*, 11 February 1913; *The Japan Times*, 13 February 1913; 'Emperor's Birthday,' *The Japan Times*, 31 August 1913; 'The Emperor's Birthday,' *The Japan Times*, 2 September 1913; 'Jimmu Tenno's Anniversary,' *The Japan Times*, 13 February 1914.
14. 'The Imperial Birthday,' *The Japan Times*, 31 August 1915.
15. 'National Era Day was Celebrated with Special Enthusiasm,' *The Japan Times*, 13 February 1916.
16. See 'The Emperor is Thirty-eight To-day,' *The Japan Times*, 31 August 1917.
17. See 'The Imperial Birthday,' *The Japan Times*, 2 September 1916; 'The Kigensetsu Celebrated,' *The Japan Times*, 13 February 1917; 'Anniversary of Founding of Japan's Imperial Line is Auspiciously Celebrated,' *The Japan Times*, 12 February 1918; 'His Majesty's 40th Birthday Celebrated with Ceremonies at the Imperial Palace,' *The Japan Times*, 1 September 1918.
18. See *The Japan Times*, 13 February 1919; *The Japan Times*, 31 August 1919; 'Nikko Rejoices on Emperor Day,' *The Japan Times*, 1 September 1920.
19. 'American Woman Writes Poem Read in Commemoration of Empire Day,' *The Japan Times*, 12 February 1921.
20. *Ibid.*
21. 'Tokyo Route of Imperial Heir Fixed,' *The Japan Times*, 31 August 1921; 'Imperial Fleet Welcomes Prince,' *The Japan Times*, 1 September 1921; 'No "Banzais" No Applause for Prince. New Police Order Places Ban on all Democratic Salutations,' *The Japan Times*, 2 September 1921; 'Forbidden "Banzais" is Roared by Millions as Crown Prince Arrives', *The Japan Times*, 3 September 1921.
22. 'Crown Prince's Odessy a Series of Welcomes,' *The Japan Times*, 3 September 1921.
23. *Ibid.*
24. *Ibid.*
25. 'His Imperial Highness,' *The Japan Times*, 3 September 1921.
26. Akira Iriye, *Across the Pacific. An Inner History of American - East Asian Relations* (Introduction by John K. Fairbank. New York 1967). pp. 143-145, 151-153; Morinosuke Kajima, *A Brief Diplomatic History of Modern Japan* (Tokyo 1965), pp. 71-75.
27. 'World Peace Japan's Desire through the Ages,' *The Japan Times*, 11 February 1922.
28. E. Shibusawa, 'Pride and Glory,' (*The Japan Times*, 26 January 1924).
29. 'The Imperial Wedding,' *The Japan Times*, 25 January 1924. See also 'Congratulations,' *The Japan Times*, 26 January 1924.
30. 'Banzai,' *The Japan Times*, 26 January 1924.
31. Setsuzo Sawada, 'Japans Today Standing at Cross Roads,' (*The Japan Times*, 26 January 1924).
32. *Ibid.*
33. 'Count Futura, Japan Now in State of Transition,' (*The Japan Times*, 26 January 1924).
34. Jinji G. Kasai, 'Japan Facing a New Era Bravely', (*The Japan Times*, 26 January 1924).
35. See also 'His Imperial Highness Had Almost Spartan Training on Advice of Great Grandsire,' *The Japan Times*, 26 January 1924.
36. See also 'Emperor Rests Quietly,' *The Japan Times*, 17 December 1926; 'Forlorn Hope is Held,' *The Japan Times*, 19 December 1926; 'Empire in Great Agony,' *The Japan Times*. 20 December 1926; 'The Nation Hushed in Supreme Solicitude,' *The Osaka Mainichi* & *Tokyo Nichi Nichi* (OM & TNN): 'His Majesty' Condition,' OM & TNN, 25 November 1926.
37. 'Passing of Emperor Marks Close of Era,' *The Japan Times*, 25 December 1926.
38. 'Glorious Era of Taishō is Closed with Death of Late Emperor Yoshihito,' *The Japan Times*, 25 December 1926.
39. *Ibid.*
40. 'National Lamentation,' *The Japan Times*, 26 December 1926.
41. *Ibid.*
42. 'Theory of Imperial Rule,' *The Japan Times*, 29 December 1926.
43. *Ibid.*
44. 'Land in Mourning,' *The Japan Times*, 24 January 1927.
45. 'Prince Regent is 124th Ruler of Island Empire,' *The Japan Times*, 25 December 1926.
46. 'Era of Radiant Peace,' *The Japan Times*, 27 December 1926.
47. See Note 11.
48. See also 'National Lamentation,' *The Japan Times*.
49. 'The Dying Year,' *The Japan Times*, 31 December 1926.
50. 'Second Year of Showa,' *The Japan Times*, 4 January 1927.
51. 'Spirit of Kigensetsu Festivity,' OM & TNN, 11 February 1926.
52. 'Critical Condition of Emperor's Health,' OM & TNN, 19 December 1926.
53. 'The Death of the Emperor,' OM & TNN, 26 December 1926.
54. 'The Imperial Obsequies,' OM & TNN, 8 February 1927.
55. 'New York Papers Praise Virtue of the Late Democratic Emperor,' OM & TNN, 26 December 1926.
56. 'New Emperor's Accession,' OM & TNN, 26 December 1926.
57. 'World Sympathises with Japan,' OM & TNN, 28 December 1926.
58. 'New Emperor's Accession,' OM & TNN, 26 December 1926.

The Batavia Conference of 1934 and its Importance to Dutch Japanese Relations in the Decade Before Pearl Harbor

BOB DE GRAAFF

On 31 May 1934, Eelco van Kleffens, then head of the Diplomatic Section of the Dutch Foreign Office and later war-time minister of Foreign Affairs, wrote that Dutch foreign policy so far had been conditioned by the conviction that both the Netherlands and the Dutch East Indies (D.E.I.) were in the centre of a cyclone, where peace and quiet prevailed amidst the turbulence of strong forces. And, he added, the Dutch government would be wise to continue its foreign policy on these suppositions.[1] Only a week later Japan and the Netherlands entered into economic negotiations in Batavia (present-day Jakarta), which would prove to be the first major shock to such self-complacent convictions.

It is my thesis that - as far as the D.E.I. are concerned - these negotiations should be made the point of departure in literature on the prelude of the Pacific War rather than the better known economic talks of 1940 and 1941. In 1934 the Japanese tried to pull the D.E.I. into their economic sphere of influence, while the Netherlands government was still fully sovereign. After the failure of this attempt, the Japanese tried again in 1940 and 1941, when Dutch territory in Europe had been occupied. And when they met, once again, with Dutch refusals, especially to deliver the amounts of oil that the Japanese demanded, forcible seizure of the East Indian archipelago seemed to be the only option to the Japanese government. So the Batavia Conference of 1934 was the first part of the Japanese 'hop-skip-jump-approach' of the D.E.I.

From the end of the nineteenth century until 1933 the Dutch had maintained an open door and a free trade policy in the D.E.I., not least to make their fragile presence in the East more acceptable to other powers. However, Japanese inroads on the Dutch East Indian economy between 1929 and 1933 seemed to make continuation of this economic policy more dangerous than its abrogation. As Meyer Ranneft, head of the Dutch delegation in Batavia in 1934, put it: 'free trade is Japanese trade' and 'the open door leads to the Japanese home.'[2] According to Hart, another member of the Dutch delegation, free trade and an open door would imply a Japanese monopoly of the East Indian economy: 'For as a matter of course the Japanese products would be transported by Japanese ships, would be cleared by Japanese storage companies, would then be distributed by Japanese retailers and would finally be sold to the consumers by Japanese shopkeepers.'[3]

Underlying the increase of Japanese exports to the D.E.I. were several factors, such as the expansion of the Japanese textile-industry for both economic and internal political reasons; the expansion of the Japanese textile-industry because of the need for foreign exchange in view of the construction of a war economy; the collapse of the Chinese market; the devaluation of the yen by over 60 per cent against the guilder in December 1931; market strategies calculated to conquer large market segments prior to obtaining profits; and the demand of the Indonesian population for low-priced commodities.

The most tangible evidence for the D.E.I. of the boom in Japanese exports was the increase in exports of textiles which made up two-thirds of Japanese exports to the D.E.I. Especially after December 1931 Japanese textile exports to the D.E.I. took on avalanche-like proportions. In the Indies, Japan's share in the import of cotton tissues rose from 27 per cent in 1929 to 77 per cent in 1934, her share in the import of rayon tissues rose even stronger, from 30 per cent to 92 per cent, thereby almost ousting the Netherlands and Great Britain from the Dutch East Indian market.[4]

During 1933 the East Indian government took several restrictive measures to protect its own industries and Dutch and other European imports against the growing stream of Japanese goods. Most important among these measures was the Crisis Import Ordinance, which made it possible to establish import quotas for certain goods. In 1933 quotas were established for cement and beer and in early 1934 for multi-coloured fabrics and bleached cottons. Secondly, a system of import licenses came under consideration that could be used to protect western import firms against Japanese competitors. Thirdly, a system of business regulation to check newcomers in certain industries was being studied. And last, regulations were developed to restrict immigration into the D.E.I.

These measures evoked strong reactions from Japan. These reactions fitted in well with Dutch prime minister Colijn's intentions to use them in order to be in a better position via-à-vis Japan for purposes of negotiating a supplement to the 1912 trade and shipping treaty between Japan and the Netherlands.[5] Thus he hoped to stabilise Japanese imports at a lower level than that of 1933 and at the same time to further D.E.I. exports to Japan, the trade balance between the two being at a 4.5:1 disadvantage to the D.E.I. Additional objectives of Colijn were to create new possibilities for the Dutch textile industry in the D.E.I. and to keep enough room for other nations' exports to the D.E.I., which then could be used to bargain for D.E.I. exports, as the global trade atmosphere was to be increasingly dominated by reciprocity on a bilateral basis.

The Japanese government accepted the invitation of the Dutch government to discuss the trade relations with the D.E.I. They urged the desirability to hold the conference in Batavia, where the British, who in the mistaken view of the Japanese were the instigators of the D.E.I. restrictive measures, would be less able to influence Dutch policy than they would be in The Hague. The Dutch government accepted Batavia as a place for the conference, in the first place because they were not fully au fait with the details of the economic situation in the D.E.I., and secondly out of fear of colonial resentment if a conference of such importance to the D.E.I. would be held in The Hague. On 3 June the Japanese delegation headed by Nagaoka Haruichi, former ambassador to Berlin and to Paris and a former legation secretary and minister to The Hague, arrived in Batavia. In a press statement at the quay of Tanjong Priok, Nagaoka reminded the Dutch that during the *sakoku* they had been in a preferential position in Japan; that the treaty of 1912 rested on the principle of free trade and the most favoured nation principle; that special relations between the Indonesians and the Japanese would be more in line with world historical developments than colonial rule by the Dutch; and that relations between the D.E.I. and Japan should be based on the principle of 'co-existence and co-prosperity.'[6] In the following days Nagaoka made it clear that he had come to talk politics.

At first the Dutch now seemed to be taken by surprise by their own initiative. From the Dutch perspective a development for the worse had taken place when, shortly before, British-Indian-Japanese trade talks is Simla had failed to produce the results desired by the Japanese. Thereafter the Japanese government was pressed by both economic reasons and Japanese nationalism to take a tough stand in Batavia.

From the Dutch point of view Batavia had been a remarkable choice as a place for the conference, since it had never been a diplomatic centre. It lacked the apparatus for treaty negotiations and the Dutch delegation had to admit that their Japanese counterparts were better prepared and better equipped than they were. Since The Hague retained the power to take the ultimate decisions, while on the other hand for the first time Dutch East Indian colonial officials formed a large part of the delegation, many frictions ensued between The Hague and Batavia. Mainly because of these frictions it took The Hague almost four months following the opening of the conference to formulate its desiderata. A major defect regarding the sensitive nature of the conference was the fact that following the failure of the London Economic and Monetary Conference, a new trade policy for the D.E.I. had not yet been developed and would be outlined only by trial and error during the Batavia Conference.

Meanwhile, their presence in the Indies gave the Japanese delegation ample opportunities for propaganda amongst the local population. Most damaging in the personal sphere was the fact that the head of the Dutch delegation, Meyer Ranneft, vice-president of the Council of the Indies, charged with previously unknown responsibilities, lost his composure in face of the Japanese intimidations and became extremely nervous. On the other hand the Dutch had the advantage of the Japanese. Just before the opening of the conference, Room 14 of the Royal Netherlands East Indian Army had succeeded in breaking the Japanese diplomatic codes, so that the Dutch delegation was informed of the messages between Nagaoka and the Gaimusho (Foreign Ministry). Thanks to this knowledge Batavia urged The Hague several times to use diplomatic channels in either The Hague or Tokyo to convey the Dutch desiderata to the Japanese government, because they knew from reading his messages that Nagaoka was misinforming his government. From the exchanges between Nagaoka and Tokyo the Dutch knew also that after their failure to produce the desired results in Simla the Japanese government was determined to bring about results in Batavia. So, when by July the Japanese were no longer rattling their sabres the Dutch could play hard to get.[7]

Despite the tropical surroundings, the atmosphere at the conference was rather chilly during the first months. Nagaoka described it to the Dutch as 'the like of which I have never experienced at the many international conferences that I have hitherto attended,'[8] to which Meyer Ranneft replied that the Dutch had formed a conception of the inauguration of a trade conference that was 'widely divergent' from the attitude adopted by the Japanese delegation.[9] In face of the propaganda amongst the Indonesians by members of the Japanese delegation, the Attorney-General even informed the Japanese delegation that, if they persevered in influencing the natives, they would be forcibly ejected, whether they claimed diplomatic status or not.[10] Such was the initial deadlock at the conference that for a while the D.E.I. authorities promulgated another quota (for pottery), while the Japanese declared a temporary export boycott to the D.E.I. of pottery and unbleached cottons.

It took until mid-September, i.e. more than three months, before the delegations could come to business. Most of the factual negotiations thereafter took place in 'private talks' between the Dutch official, Van Gelderen, and the Japanese consul-general in Batavia, Koshida, in which prestige played a less prominent role than in the formal meetings between Meyer Ranneft and Nagaoka. From then on it was Dutch policy to see that if the conference ended prematurely, this should result from a mutual recognition by both parties of the impracticability of coming to an agreement.[11]

There were two major obstacles at the conference. First, the Dutch were willing to maintain Japanese imports at a high level only if Japan would increase imports from the D.E.I. The D.E.I. wanted especially to export large amounts of sugar, for which Japan should give a guarantee of no re-export. Thanks to sugar production in Formosa, however, Japan had become almost self-sufficient in sugar by 1928. The Japanese were more interested in strategic raw materials, among them rubber and quinine in such quantities, that their export would conflict with D.E.I. export restrictions of these commodities. A second obstacle was the Dutch insistence to discuss shipping at the conference, which the Japanese delegation doggedly refused, since the Japanese and Dutch shipping companies had virtually reached agreement at the time of the opening of the Batavia conference.

In mid-December it was decided to postpone the conference until the private shipping companies finalised an agreement that would then have to be endorsed by both governments. This came about in July 1936, whereafter in 1937 and 1938 trade agreements were concluded, whereby the by then reduced figures of Japanese exports to the D.E.I. were accepted by both parties.

After the postponement of the conference in December 1934 the Dutch East Indian government had felt free to enact several new restrictive measures, which led to a decline in Japanese imports from 32 per cent of total D.E.I. imports in 1934 to 27 per cent in 1936 and even further to 14 per cent in 1938 (although the latter figure was partly caused by the Japanese involvement in China). The economic defence of the D.E.I. seemed to be an outstanding success.

After the conference the D.E.I. government had felt confident to take such restrictive measures, because they had come to the conclusion that Japanese aggression against the Indies would not be dependent on disagreeable economic measures, but on Japan's evaluation of her relations with the major powers, and that Japanese aggression would be unlikely as long as there were no serious troubles in Europe. At the end of a comprehensive report on the negotiations in 1934 the Dutch delegation concluded: 'Moreover it is worth noting that just because until now we did not lose during the negotiations, this must have brought home to the Japanese the thought that it is impossible for them ...to propose to "help" us in a "friendly" way to develop the Indies. The Netherlands sovereignty is a hindrance to the materialisation of the Japanese ideal which they hope to achieve by peaceful means. This has become more evident than ever before. This is not to detract from the present peacefulness of the Japanese, but we are well advised never to lose sight of the Japanese ideals regarding the Indies.'[12]

That the Dutch delegation had indeed frustrated the Japanese by their self-praised stubbornness might be indicated by a comment in the *Asahi Shimbun* in September 1935 referring to Nagaoka's experiences. It said that the Japanese should realise that the Dutch were the most laconic negotiators in the world: 'They are indifferent to reality; only the questions of principle of a case matter to them, even if it takes months of negotiating. Their juggling with figures and their chaffering with lots of minor details is common knowledge and is known as "Dutch account." Their conduct is hair-raising, even to Jewish businessmen, although those are quite good at it themselves.'[13]

It took only seven years to bring reality home to the Dutch. From the end of 1934 the D.E.I., pushing back Japanese imports without evoking major new Japanese protests, were experiencing their Indian Summer.

NOTES

1. General States Archives, The Hague (GSA), Foreign Office (FO), A-194/207 (Kellogg Treaty), Memorandum from Van Kleffens to De Graeff [31] May 1934.
2. GSA, File Meyer Ranneft No. 93, 'The negotiations with Japan (June-December 1934),' 31 January 1935.

3. GSA, File Meyer Ranneft, No. 98, 'Notes concerning the Japanese penetration into the D.E.I. and the trade relations between the D.E.I. and Japan since 1933,' 22 February 1936; A.C.D. de Graeff (ed.), *Van vriend tot vijand. De betrekkingen tusschen Nederlandsch-Indië em Japan*, Amsterdam 1945, 184.

4. F. M. van Asbeck, '*Les responsabilités néerlandaises dans le Pacifique*, Paris [1939], 222; T. Nagaoka, *Japanese trade and industry. Present and future*. London 1936, 562.

5. GSA, Ministry of the Colonies (MinCol), V14-10-1933-D24, Colijn to De Jonge, 14 October 1933; V12-1-1934-M1, Colijn to De Jonge, 12 January 1934; Public Record Office, Kew, (PRO), FO 371/18566, W 3831/86/29, Sir H. Montgomery to Foreign Office, 21 April 1934.

6. GSA, File Meyer Ranneft, No. 93, 'The negotiations with Japan (June-December 1934),' 31 January 1935, enclosure.

7. R. D. Haslach, *Nish: no kaze, hare. Nederlands-Indische inlichtingendienst contra agressor Japan*, Weesp 1985, 80-88; Joh. de Vries (ed.), *E. Heldring. Herinneringen en Dagboek (1871-1954)*, II, Groningen 1972, 1080.

8. GSA, MinCol, V3-8-1934-Q21, De Jonge to Colijn 30 July 1934.

9. Diplomatic Record Office Tokyo, B 2-0-0 J/N 2-1-1, Meyer Ranneft to Nagaoka, 2 August 1934.

10. PRO, FO 371/18572, W9829/90/29, R. V. Laming to Sir H. Mongomery, 1 November 1934.

11. GSA, MinCol, V4-12-1934-E34, Colijn to Queen Wilhelmina, 4 December 1934; File De Jonge, No. 15, Colijn to De Jonge, 5 December 1934; PRO, FO 371/18572, W8883/90/29, H. Fitzmaurice to Department of Overseas Trade, 25 September 1934.

12. GSA, File Meyer Ranneft, No. 93, 'The negotiations with Japan (June-December 1934),' 31 January 1935; No. 98, 'Notes concerning the Japanese penetration into the D.E.I. and the trade relations between the D.E.I. and Japan since 1933.' 22 February 1936.

13. *Asahi Shimbun* 14 September 1935, quoted in: Foreign Office, Legation Tokyo 1900-1941, box 43, Geheim 80A.

Admiral Yonai Mitsumasa as Navy Minister (1937-39) - Dove or Hawk?

GERHARD KREBS

THE PROBLEM

Yonai Mitsumasa (1880-1948), who became one of Japan's most prominent naval officers, was born in the northern prefecture of Iwate and graduated from Morioka Middle School, the Naval Academy and the Naval Staff College. An expert on gunnery, he was stationed in Russia (1915-17) as well as in Germany (1920-22). After several commands in the fleet and in the naval yards, and after service on the navy staff, he was appointed Commander of the Combined Fleet with the rank of vice admiral in 1936. In February of the following year he became navy minister, being promoted to full admiral shortly thereafter. He retained this post until August 1939, during the Hayashi, the first Konoe and the Hiranuma cabinets. In January 1940 he entered the reserve in order to form a cabinet of his own. This government collapsed half a year later due to pressure by the army, which aimed at closer connexions with the then prevailing military power, Germany. After reentering active service, he became navy minister again in July 1944 under prime minister Koiso and continued in that post during the Suzuki cabinet until Japan's surrender. He also served in the same capacity in the post-war Higashikuni and Shidehara governments until December 1945, when concomitant to the dissolution of the armed forces the navy ministry was abolished together with the army ministry.

Historians usually regard Yonai as a moderate, pro-western politician with liberal leanings, who opposed aggressive army policies firmly and did not compromise with the young radicals in the navy. Belonging to the anti-war faction he is supposed to have struggled to avoid an alliance with the Axis powers and a policy of military expansion.[1] He is thought to have acted in unison with Yamamoto Isoroku, who was his vice minister until April 1938, and Inoue Shigeyoshi, chief of the influential military bureau in the navy ministry. Yonai is seldom reckoned among the radicals and expansionists.[2] His image was formed largely by the attitude he displayed during his time as navy minister in the 1930s. However, the usual characterisation of his policies contradicts the often-cited theory that a willingness to compromise with other power groups and one's own subordinates is an important aspect of the Japanese social and political system. So, if Yonai, in fact, had ignored the younger naval officers' views and stubbornly opposed the policy promoted by the army, he would have committed a breach of loyalty and would have been acting in a way contrary to Japanese rules of conduct. Therefore, the usual assumption about Yonai's policy will be questioned in the light of the three most important problems that arose during his first tenure of office as navy minister: 1. The China War; 2. The beginning of the Southern advance; 3. An alliance with the Axis powers.

THE CHINA WAR

Not much is known about the taciturn Yonai's political ideas previous to his becoming navy minister, but the outbreak of the China War in July 1937 forced him to take a position. In the beginning he opposed Army Minister Sugiyama's demand for the dispatch of reenforcements and won the support of Prime Minister Konoe and Foreign Minister Hirota in his attempt to avoid an extension of the conflict, seeking a local solution instead.[3] On 11 July, however, only four days after the outbreak of hostilities, he agreed with the other cabinet members to the dispatch of three divisions from Japan in order to speed up a solution, with the proviso that the principle of non-extension would be observed.[4] The army had to pay a price for the navy's consent: on the same day the Army General Staff approved the Navy General Staff's proposal to dispatch troops to Shanghai as well as to Tsingtao, if Japanese nationals were endangered due to rising anti-Japanese sentiments.[5] This agreement, based upon an interservice arrangement from October the previous year,[6] required the consent of the army ministry. Therefore, Yonai pressed Army Minister Sugiyama who answered evasively.[7]

At this point in time the China incident had nearly been settled without the dispatch of Japanese reenforcements. The navy long entertained a policy of gaining control over Shanghai as well as over large areas of Central and South China, which led to full-scale war. When a Japanese naval officer and a seaman were killed in Shanghai on 9 August, Yonai requested the cabinet to dispatch two army divisions to that Chinese city and to make preparations for the conquest of Nanking.

As had happened previously in 1932 in connexion with the Manchurian Incident, the navy again became the driving force behind the extension of hostilities into the city of Shanghai. The Navy High Command decided to solve the problem by force; Yonai explained the situation to the cabinet on 10 August, and requested a mobilisation plan.[8] The army was reluctant, since it was primarily concerned with defending against the USSR and restricting the fighting in North China, but it had to give in due to the former interservice agreements.[9] The cabinet decided on 12 August to dispatch two army divisions to Shanghai in order to back the marines there. Several days later the Japanese navy, approaching the Chinese coast, became the target of the Chinese air force; it then shelled Nanking as well as other Chinese sea and river ports.

In an emergency cabinet session on the evening of 14 August, Yonai showed his determination to follow a more radical path. Against the recommendation of Foreign Minister Hirota he advocated and procured a strongly worded government statement, to be published the following day, delineating decisive steps which would cause China to reconsider its attitude. When Finance Minister Kaya warned that an extension of the war would cause great difficulties for the Japanese economy, Yonai condemned his weak attitude without letting him finish his explanations. Finally the Finance Minister conceded. Yonai then turned to Army Minister Sugiyama and demanded the conquest of Nanking, the Chinese capital. The general pointed out the necessity of preparing for operations against the USSR and doubted the wisdom of occupying Nanking, which would be of no value for Japan. He further warned that such a campaign would involve the Empire ever more in an extended war. Yonai, however, adhered to his demand. The Tenno (Emperor) was shocked by the radical attitude the navy had displayed and admonished the minister during a personal meeting not to be overcome by his own emotions.[10]

Extension of the war was advantageous for the navy in that the opposition to enlarging the fleet and its air branch was silenced. In return the navy approved the army's demand for economic mobilisation laws and an increase in active duty divisions. Moreover, the war enabled the navy to fulfil step by step its old dream of a 'Southern advance' (nanshin). At first, it gradually imposed a blockade of Chinese shipping over the entire coast. At the beginning of September the navy occupied the Chinese island of Pratas, situated about 300 km south-east of Hong Kong. Protests by the USA, Britain and France had no effect.

The China War was also seen as a chance to bring about the navy's plan for an annexation of the island of Hainan formulated in September of the previous year. At that time the scheme had failed because of army resistance; the Foreign Ministry, too, had expressed opposition, because foreign powers had shown great concern.[11] Now the Japanese navy appeared off Hainan and shelled the coast. The western powers feared not only an occupation of Hainan, but also of the Paracel islands, situated off the coast of French-Indochina.[12]

From the beginning, influential members of the Army General Staff had regarded with great concern the hostilities in China and the continuous extension of the fighting. They feared involvement in a long war which would endanger their armament plans for war against the USSR. They brought about attempts of mediation through Germany which as the sole great power had maintained good relations with Japan as well as China. The conditions stipulated by the Army General Staff were changed by the Army, Navy and Foreign Ministry, thereby becoming more unfavourable for China, and approved by the Inner Cabinet. But they were transmitted to China via Germany at the end of October only in an incomplete version.[13] Chiang Kai-shek, hoping for support from the western powers, delayed his answer.

In November Shanghai fell after fierce fighting. At the end of the month the Nine Power Conference on the China War ended without any practical results. On 13 December the Japanese completed their conquest of Nanking, having met surprisingly little resistance. Three days later the navy occupied the island of Quemoy, situated off the important harbour of Amoy, extending its control over the Chinese coast many hundreds of kilometres to the south. The Foreign Ministry, which had restrained the navy's expansion policy in previous years, now supported this policy and laid claim to the Spratly Islands, an archipelago situated between the Philippines, Borneo and French-Indochina. It was unclear to whom the islands belonged and the Japanese - i.e. mainly the navy's - claim had strained relations with France for several years.[14]

In the army, too, the position of the hawks was strengthened. The Army Ministry under Sugiyama gained influence at the expense of the General Staff and formulated more severe peace conditions for China. These became the guiding principles of army policy.[15] On 21 December the cabinet decided on eleven conditions which left only a kind of colonial status for China under Japanese rule.[16] The details were never made known to China, due to an intrigue by Foreign Minister Hirota. He secured cabinet approval to his plan that it would be left up to Hirota himself as to how the Japanese claims would be transmitted;[17] moreover, he would not disclose the details of the conditions.[18] Hirota gave only a general explanation to the German ambassador and demanded that China accept immediately all Japanese conditions. Berlin's representative was shocked, and after several meetings, succeeded in receiving permission to transmit at least Hirota's oral explanations to China and in having the deadline extended.[19]

The policy of the Japanese government at that time was aimed at establishing puppet regimes in China and therefore refusing recognition of Chiang as the sole ruler of the country. Cabinet decisions, which had been taken behind the back of Army and Navy General Staff, had been fully supported by Navy Minister Yonai. The Army General Staff, however, was informed by the German military attaché, that the eleven points had never been transmitted, and it exerted pressure on the foreign ministry to inform Chiang about the Japanese conditions.[20] Moreover, it demanded the convening of an Imperial Conference, the first since the Russian-Japanese War. The Foreign Ministry and the Navy Ministry resisted for some time but eventually had to yield. The Imperial Conference was held on 11 January 1938. The chiefs of staff pleaded for the conclusion of a generous peace and the adherence to the eleven conditions.[21]

It seems doubtful there was any chance for a 'generous peace:' China had been shocked by the conditions, which it had come to know only in a vague form.[22] The Imperial Conference, however, resulted in another extension of time for Chiang's answer as well as in a series of liaison conferences (between the Imperial Headquarters and the government) and cabinet sessions. The rift between the staffs and the cabinet remained and became even deeper, when an answer from China arrived on 14 January: Chiang wished to be informed exactly about the Japanese conditions.[23] While the cabinet refused to continue the peace initiative, Headquarters demanded another liaison conference,[24] which convened the next morning and continued deep in the night with heavy arguing. Again the representatives of the government including Navy Minister Yonai demanded an end to the negotiations, which the chiefs and vice-chiefs of staff refused.[25] When Hirota denied that China had any desire for peace, he was supported by Yonai, who declared, the foreign minister had the full confidence of the government and there would be no way out except for the cabinet to resign, if headquarters should question Hirota's integrity.[26] At this point the conference was interrupted and the army and navy staffs consulted about whether the peace initiative should be broken off or the cabinet toppled. It was concluded that the resignation of the government would reveal the discord among Japan's leaders to their own people as well as to other nations with negative results. Therefore both staffs agreed, though warning repeatedly of the probable consequences, to declare Chiang's 'non-recognition.'[27] Therefore, one must say that Yonai's blackmail had been successful. On the following day the Japanese government issued a public statement saying it would cease henceforth to deal with the regime of Chiang Kai-shek.

THE SOUTHERN ADVANCE

With the continuation of the war secured in early 1938, the navy intensified its preparation for an advance into Southern China. It planned to use this area as a base for further expansion into South-East Asia. Those plans, aiming above all at the occupation of the Dutch Indies with its rich oilfields, had already been made after the first Shanghai Incident in 1932.[28] Control over Taiwan, annexed by Japan in 1895, played an important role in the navy's policy. In 1936 an inactive admiral, Kobayashi Seizo, took over the governorship of the island, which was held until 1945 by a navy officer. Also in 1936 the navy tried for the first time to occupy Hainan, but had to retreat in face of army opposition. Though the navy's intention was, 'to circumscribe Britain's position in East Asia,'[29] the first victim obviously would be France, whose zone of interest in South China and possession of Indochina would be endangered by Japanese control over Hainan.[30] Paris also feared the occupation of the Paracels and the Spratlys. Under heavy pressure, for which it held the Imperial Navy responsible, France had been obliged in October 1937, to close the military supply route to the Chinese Nationalists through Indochina.[31]

The bombing of Hainan by the Japanese navy air force, anti-French campaigns in Tokyo, and the appearance of Japanese citizens on the Paracels[32] caused France to act. In early July 1938 it occupied the islands and prepared a similar action for the Spratlys.[33] Japan claiming to govern China, protested against the annexation of the Paracels as Chinese territory.[34]

In the spring of 1938 the navy had made use of its control over Taiwan, installing within the governor's administration its own bureau for elaborating expansion plans. The object of its plans was first Hainan and the provinces of Southern China, and eventually all South-East Asia.[35] In September 1938 the navy once again demanded the conquest of Hainan, but failed again because of stiff army opposition.[36] The foreign minister, Hirota, and later his successor Ugaki, did not, however, exclude an annexation of Hainan in conversations with the British ambassador.[37] Other evidence also indicates the navy gradually had won over the Foreign Ministry to its policy of Southern advance. So, for example, it received permission to bomb the railway going from Indochina into China at the end of 1938,[38] though it delayed initiating this action repeatedly. Finally the delay lasted a whole year.

Yonai endeavoured during this time in cabinet sessions and liaison conferences to get consent for the navy's policy. On 25 November 1938 his vigorous demands for a conquest of Hainan succeeded at a Five Minister Conference, and the occupation of the island became official policy.[39] It was carried out by navy and army troops in February 1939. In March of that year the occupation of the Spratlys (Shin nan gunto) followed, as had been decided in a cabinet session on 23 December 1938.[40] Hainan and the Spratlys as well as Pratas and the Paracels were officially put under the administration of the governor of Taiwan.

THE QUESTION OF A TRIPARTITE ALLIANCE

During 1938 it became obvious to Japan that China would not surrender and that instead the war would lead to conflicts with other powers. To deter other nations from becoming involved, an idea originated in the army calling for the conclusion of a defence alliance with Germany and Italy. Both were already linked loosely with Tokyo by the Anticomintern Pact. While the proposal was welcomed in Berlin and Rome, opinions were divided in Japan. The army agreed with the European Axis powers to conclude a treaty against all possible enemies, but the Navy and the Foreign Ministry intended only an alliance against the Soviet Union, though exerting pressure against the western powers was also considered. Soon it should become obvious, however, that there was a deep rift in the navy. While the leaders of the ministry - Yonai, Yamamoto and Inoue - took a reserved attitude, many of their subordinates - and in the Navy Staff even the majority - pleaded for a full alliance in accord with the proposal of Germany and the Japanese army. The leader of this movement was Captain Oka Takazumi, chief of the first division of the Military Affairs Bureau in the Navy Ministry.[41] He arranged a meeting between Yonai and War Minister Itagaki in August 1938 which was to be followed by a whole series of meetings in the next months.[42] Both ministers were born in the remote prefecture of Iwate, liked to drink, and during their informal talks seem to have developed good personal relations.

The dialogue thus begun resulted in conferences between representatives of the Army, Navy and Foreign Ministry producing a compromise draft.[43] Out of regard for differing points of view, however, the formulation was so vague, that every party involved could interpret the terms as it liked. That became the origin of a political crisis which lasted a whole year. Even when the wording was changed again and again, the army - likewise the Japanese ambassadors in Berlin and Rome - claimed, that it meant a full alliance, while the foreign and the navy ministers insisted that Britain, France and America were not contemplated as potential enemies. On the other hand the Navy General Staff and a large part of the navy ministry soon sided with the army and followed its interpretation.[44] Yonai was eventually forced to compromise. When the Japanese ambassadors in the Axis capitals simply refused to submit a new draft in January 1939 which did not clearly oblige Japan to provide military assistance against the western powers, Foreign Minister Arita insisted on adhering to the original formulation, but had to give in, when War Minister Itagaki and Navy Minister Yonai opposed him unanimously and demanded a new compromise taking into consideration the wishes of the two ambassadors.[45] Yonai, who had already promised to support his army colleague on the evening previous to this Five Minister Conference,[46] seems to have tried to save the unity of the navy as well as the cabinet.

In search of a compromise, the radical middle echelons of the navy drafted a new proposal very similar to the army's. It further limited Japan's options vis-à-vis the western powers. Yonai, who presented this new plan to a Five Minister Conference on 18 March, met with stiff resistance from Arita.[47] Several days later it was decided to present to the Axis powers first the original proposal, and if this was rejected, second a compromise drafted by the Foreign Ministry. Should this be rejected also, a plan, obviously based on the navy and the army outline, was to be proposed.[48] When the ambassadors in the Axis capitals flatly refused to present a draft including any reservations, the situation in the Japanese government changed: Yonai now sided with Arita and both compelled the army at the end of April to agree to a new proposal that the Japanese plan be transmitted by the Axis ambassadors in Tokyo to their governments., Japan should be exempted from any obligation of automatic military assistance immediately after the outbreak of hostilities.[49] Arita's and Yonai's fighting spirit was aroused even more and their bonds strengthened when shortly after ambassador Oshima in Berlin made an unauthorised promise of Japanese intervention in the event of war on the German side. He sent his own compromise draft to Tokyo which elicited the understanding of War Minister Itagaki and Prime Minister Hiranuma.[50]

Navy Vice Minister Yamamoto even gave an interview to the press denouncing further compromises in the negotiations with Germany, which still were secret, and criticised the attitude of Hiranuma and Itagaki.[51] It seems that he looked with mistrust on Yonai's efforts to establish a common course with the army. Similarly, vice admiral Inoue Shigeyoshi tried to undermine the alliance.[52] Yonai, however, still sought a compromise with Itagaki, and held further meetings with him.[53] The Navy Minister's attitude and his vague statements were the chief cause of the unclear decision made at the Five Minister Conference on 20 May.[54] In the resulting controversy, when the army maintained that an unrestricted alliance had been approved, even the emperor sided with Yonai and Arita: he ordered the army to adhere to the March decision.[55]

Yonai continued to seek a compromise and renewed his talks with Itagaki,[56] but the problem of an alliance was not made the subject of any cabinet sessions or liaison conferences for about two months. When Itagaki on 8 August at a Five Minister Conference surprisingly demanded the conclusion of an unrestricted tripartite pact without delay, all the other members opposed him vehemently.[57] A cabinet crisis was the result, but the expected resignation of War Minister Itagaki did not take place. In this situation news arrived on 22 August that Germany and the Soviet Union were going to conclude a non-aggression pact. The members of Hiranuma's cabinet were terribly shocked and resigned.

CONCLUSION

Navy Minister Yonai had acted fully in accordance with Japanese rules of conduct, as he strove to take into account the views of his more radical subordinates. He tried to position himself between the younger officers and the more cautious admirals Yamamoto and Inoue, because it had become obvious that he could not ignore the demands of the middle echelon group. Following a middle course he was able to avoid an open rupture within the navy.

Equally, Yonai behaved towards other power groups, especially the army, in compliance with Japanese ways of decision-making. Through intensive talks with Itagaki he sought a compromise with the army and temporarily risked the estrangement not only of Foreign Minister Arita but also Yamamoto and Inoue. He thereby succeeded, at least temporarily, in reducing tensions within the Japanese leadership and avoided a cabinet resignation.

With respect to the question of whether Yonai was a dove or a hawk, one has to consider the two developments which had produced the necessity of seeking an alliance with Germany and Italy: the China War and the beginning of the Southern advance. In both cases Yonai played an active role, pushing through his policies in the cabinet and the liaison conferences. He silenced the more moderate Navy General Staff in the discussions about a settlement of the China War and triumphed over the Army General Staff. Far from being one of the most radical officers in the navy he always took a middle position, which means, he was just 'normal,' but under the conditions of the 1930s that implies, he was rather hawk than dove.

NOTES

1. See e.g. Takagi Sokichi, Yamamoto Isoroku to Yonai Mitsumasa. Tokyo, 1950; Takagi Sokichi, Jidenteki Nihon kaigun shimatsuki. Tokyo, 1971; Ogata Taketora, Ichi gunjin no shogai. Kaiso no Yonai Mitsumasa. Tokyo, 1955; Takamiya Tahei, Yonai Mitsumasa. Tokyo, 1958; Agawa Hiroyuki, Yamamoto Isoroku. Tokyo 1965 (engl. The Reluctant Admiral. Yamamoto and the Imperial Navy. Tokyo, 1979); Agawa Hiroyuki, Yonai Mitsumasa. 2 Vols., Tokyo, 1978; Sanematsu Yuzuru, Yonai Mitsumasa. Tokyo, 1979; Asada Sadao, 'The Japanese Navy and the United States,' in: Dorothy Borg and Shumpei Okamoto, Eds., Pearl Harbor as History. Japanese-American Relations 1931-1941. New York, 1973, pp. 225-260.
2. Stephen E. Pelz, Race to Pearl Harbor. The Failure of the Second Naval Conference and the Onset of World War II. Cambridge/Mass., 1974, pp. 214-215; Gerhard Krebs, Japans Deutschlandpolitik 1935-1941. 2 Vols., Hamburg, 1984, esp. chapters II, III. Arthur J. Marder (Old Friends, New

Enemies: the Royal Navy and the Imperial Japanese Navy. Strategic Illusions, 1936-1941. Oxford, 1981, pp. 106-107) challenges Pelz' view claiming that Yonai only 'envisaged a southward expansion that would be achieved peacefully.' Marder writes on Yonai's role concerning the China War: '...he made clear his dislike for the China War and said it should be stopped. But he lacked the power to do so. He was only the Navy Minister, and the Navy did not have the muscle of the Army, which was doing most of the fighting' (p. 96). Yonai's aggressive attitude during the China War is at least partially dealt with by Ikeda Kiyoshi, Kaigun to Nihon. Tokyo, 1981, pp. 99-103; Usui Katsumi, Nit-Chu sense to gunbu, in: Miyake Masaki et al., eds., Showashi no gunbu to seiji. Vol. 4, Tokyo, 1983, pp. 57-88, esp. 71-72.

3. Kazami Akira, Konoe Naikaku. Tokyo, 1951, pp. 29-34; Nihonkokusaiseijigakkai Taiheiyosensogeninkenkyubu hen, Taiheiyosenso e no michi. Kaisen gaikoshi. Vol. 4, Nit-Chu senso (I), Tokyo, 1963, p. 8 (henceforth: TSM); Ogata, p. 24.

4. Kazami pp. 34-35; Hata Ikuhiko, Nit-Chu sensoshi, Tokyo, 1972, p. 202.

5. Boeicho Boeikenshujo Senshishitsu. Daihonei Rikugunbu (1), Showa jugonen gogatsu made (Senshi sosho, Vol. 8). Tokyo, 1969, pp. 438-439.

6. Hata pp. 98-99.

7. Senshi Sosho 8, pp. 453-454.

8. See the documents included in Gendaishi Shiryo, Vol. 9, Nit-Chu senso (2), Tokyo, 1964, pp. 192-198 (henceforth: GS 9).

9. On the navy's role in extending the fighting into the Shanghai area see also the recollections of Ishiwara Kanji from 1939. Though partisan, the observations have to be considered essentially correct: Ishiwara Kanji chujo kaiso otoroku, in: GS 9, pp. 302-317, esp 307-308.

10. Shimada Toshihiko bunsho - kaigun gunreibu kankei shiryo, Vol. 49 (collection held at Tokyo University, Institute of Social Science).

11. TSM 3, pp. 199-206; GS 8, pp. 217-218; Matsumoto Shunichi and Nakaoka Shinjiro, Nanshin mondai. Tokyo, 1973, pp. 18-19 (Kajima Heiwa Kankyujo hen, Nihon gaikoshi, Vol. 22).

12. Matsumoto pp. 19-20; Foreign Relations of the United States, 1937, III, Washington, 1954, pp. 523-525.

13. Tel. Dirksen to Berlin, 3 Nov. 1937, Akten zur Deutschen Auswartigen Politik, Series D, Vol. 1, Baden-Baden, 1950, No. 514 (henceforth: ADAP).

14. TSM 6 (Nanpo shinshutsu) pp. 8-9, 14; Matsumoto pp. 31-32; see also the documents included in: Documents Diplomatiques Francais, Series II, Vol. 7, Paris, 1972, No. 444; Vol. 8, No. 244; Vol. 9, Nos. 333, 473 (henceforth: DDF).

15. Official diary of the Army General Staff, Senshi Sosho 86 (Shinajihen rikugun sakusen 1), p. 468; text of the army drafts, approved 15 Dec. 1937, in GS 9, pp. 54-58.

16. Text in Gaimushō hen, Nihon gaikō nenpyo narabi ni shuyō bunsho. Vol. 2, Tokyo, 1966, pp. 380-381. Among the conditions were: de jure recognition of 'Manchukuo;' demilitarisation of North and Central China and Inner Mongolia, temporary stationing of Japanese troops in those areas and in Greater Shanghai; establishment of a new regime in North China and an anti-communist regime in Inner Mongolia; economic cooperation with Japan and Manchukuo; reparation of war costs. Furthermore, an armistice would become effective only after the conclusion of a treaty based on the above conditions.

17. Horiba Kazuo, Shina jihen sonsōshidōshi. Tokyo, 1973, p. 120.

18. Kido Kōichi Nikki. Vol. 1, Tokyo, 1966, p. 611.

19. Tel. Dirksen to Berlin, 23, 28, 29, 30 Dec. 1937 and 12 Jan. 1938, ADAP D 1, Nos. 540, 541, 546, 547, 550; Tel. Dirksen to Berlin 6 Jan. 1938, Joachim Peck, Kolonialismus ohne Kolonien. Der deutsche Imperialismus and China 1937. East Berlin, 1961, p. 163. See also Ishii Itarō, Gaikōkan no isshō. Tai-chūgoku gaikō no kaisō. Tokyo, 1972, p. 264.

20. Official diary of the Army General Staff, Senshi Sōsho 86, p. 467; Horiba p. 121.

21. Horiba pp. 125-126.

22. Tel. Trautmann to Berlin, 26 Dec., ADAP D I, No. 544.

23. Tel. Trautmann to Berlin, 13 Jan. 1938, *ibid*. No. 552; Tel. Dirksen to Berlin, 14 Jan. 1938, *ibid*. No. 553; Senshi Sōsho 86, p. 474; Ishii p. 265.

24. Official diary of the Army General Staff, Senshi Sōsho 86, p. 474; Ishii p. 265.

25. Concerning this last conference on 15 January, see the official diary of the Army General Staff, Senshi Sōsho 86, p. 475; Ishii p. 265.

26. Official diary of the Army General Staff, Senshi Sōsho 86, p. 475. According to Harada, genrō Saionji's secretary, Yonai had demanded that either the Army General Staff or the government would have to resign (Harada Kumao, Saionji-kō to seikyoku. Vol. 6, Tokyo, 1951, p. 207).

27. Official diary of the Army General Staff, Senshi Sōsho 86, p. 475; Horiba pp. 129-131; Kawabe Torashirō's recollections in GS 12, p. 446.

28. See e.g. the plan of 25 Sept. 1933 in GS 8, pp. 9-10.

29. GS 10, p. LXXXIX.

30. Japanese occupation of Hainan would have cut off the French leased territory of Kwanchou with its navy base, situated on the Liuchow peninsula just opposite Hainan. France held these rights since 1898, when also a treaty, still in force in the 1930s, was concluded, that China would not cede Hainan to another power. The French embassy in Tokyo reported with amazing accuracy the navy's expansion

plans in 1936 and its pressure on other power groups. See the documents in DDF II, 2, No. 221; DDF II, 3, Nos. 129, 295.

31. Matsumoto p. 36; Documents in DDF II, 6, No. 493; *ibid.*, 7, Nos. 19, 134, 147, 202, 308.

32. Documents in DDF II, 8, Nos. 389, 453; *ibid.*, 10, Nos. 56, 60, 139; FRUS 1938, III, p. 218.

33. DDF, II, 9, No. 536; *Ibid.*, 10, Nos. 128, 133, 162, 397; *ibid.*, 12, 426, 433; Matsumoto pp. 23-26.

34. *Ibid.* pp. 26-27; DDF II, 10, No. 173.

35. GS 10, pp. XCI, 423-464.

36. TSM 6, p. 9.

37. Documents in FRUS 1938, III, pp. 82-83, 207; Matsumoto p. 23.

38. *Ibid.* p. 47.

39. TSM 6, p. 9; GS 9, p. 359 (Hashimoto Gun chujo kaiso otoroku).

40. TSM 6, p. 14; Unno Yoshiro, 1930nendai ni okeru Nansa gunto (Shinnan gunto) no ryoyu o meguru Nich-Futsu funso. In: Seiji Kaizaishigaku, No. 200, Jan.-March 1983, pp. 39-49, esp. p. 47; R. T. Phillips, The Japanese Occupation of Hainan. In: *Modern Asian Studies*, Vol. 14, 1980, pp. 93-109. Concerning the History of the disputed islands see: Dieter Heinzig. Disputed islands in the South China Sea: Paracels - Spratiys - Pratas Wiesbaden, 1976; Marwyn S. Samuels, Contest for the South China Sea. New York, 1982; Werner Draguhn (Ed.), Umstrittene Seengebiete in Ost- und Südostasien. Das internationale Seerecht und seine regionale Bedeutung. Hamburg, 1985. Hamburg, 1985.

41. Yonai and Yamamoto formulated their opposition to a full alliance in six provocative questions, written out and handed over to Oka on 19 August 1938 (GS 10, p. 174). Oka replied quickly in written form on the next day, arguing and citing many examples to show that England would take a weak stand only if Japan maintained a resolute attitude. The best way to do this was the conclusion of a military alliance with the Axis powers (*ibid.* pp. 174-177).

42. *Ibid.* p. 174. See also Yonai's own record of the conversation of 21 August 1938 in Ogata pp. 40-43, erroneously dated August 1939.

43. Approved at Five Minister Conference 26 August, text in GS 10, p. 179.

44. *Ibid.* pp. 183-185; Showashi no Tenno. Vol. 21, Tokyo, 1973, pp. 330-339.

45. Navy document in Showashi no Tenno 23, pp. 13-14; Arita Hachiro, Bakahachi to hito wa iu. Tokyo, 1959, pp. 95-96 (where the Five Minister Conference is dated incorrectly as 13 March instead of 10 March 1939). On Foreign Minister Arita's complaints concerning Yonai's attitude toward the army see also Harada 7, pp. 326, 329.

46. Navy document in Showashi 23, p. 11.

47. GS 10, pp. 229-231; Gaimusho Gaikoshiryokan, Iwayuru bokyo kyotei kyokamondai ni kansuru zen Arita gaimudaijin shuki (henceforth: Arita Shuki). The army draft (GS 10, pp. 231-232), which was very similar to the navy plan, was presented later, but the date cannot be verified from the documents.

48. Five Minister Conference decision 22 March 1939, and related documents in GS 10, p. 234-237.

49. Navy document in Showashi no Tenno 23, p. 206. The new proposal was handed over to the Axis ambassadors in Tokyo, see tel. Ott to Berlin, 5 May 1939, ADAP D VI, No 326.

50. GS 10, pp. 270-275; Harada 7, pp. 353-355, 361f; Arita p. 101.

51. GS 10, p. 276; Showashi no Tenno 24, p. 55.

52. GS 10, pp. 227-228.

53. *Ibid.* p. 297; Navy document in Showashi no Tenno 24, pp. 170-171; Arita Shuki.

54. Showashi no Tenno 24, pp. 179-183.

55. Zoku. Gendaishi shiryo, Vol. 4, Rikugun - Hata Shunroku nisshi. Tokyo, 1983, p. 201.

56. So e.g. on 30 June (GS 10, p. 327). On 18 July, Yonai received a long letter from Itagaki dealing with the alliance problem (*ibid.* pp. 331-337).

57. *Ibid.* pp. 165, 336, 360; Ogata pp. 57-58; Harada 8, pp. 42-44.

Japanese Occupation Policy in Singapore, 1942-5

OTABE YUJI

I: STUDIES ON THE GREATER EAST ASIA CO-PROSPERITY SPHERE IN JAPAN

When Japan began the Pacific war the term, *Daitoa Senso*, or the Greater East Asia war, was used to describe the Sino-Japanese and Pacific conflicts. Japan announced that South-East Asia would be freed from European and American control by this war and that the *Daitoa Kyoeiken* or Greater East Asia Co-Prosperity Sphere would be constructed. But Japan's real goal was the acquisition of raw materials from South-East Asia with which to win the Sino-Japanese war. Japan did not aim to make South-East Asia free. During the war, not only allied prisoners but also ordinary people who lived in South-East Asia were killed. Overseas Chinese were treated with particular cruelty.

This paper will endeavour to clarify Japanese occupation policy in Singapore between 1942 and 1945 in order to understand Japanese war crimes against native peoples living in Singapore. First of all, observations will be made concerning studies in Japan examining the Greater East Asia Co-Prosperity Sphere in Japan. After World War II many Japanese scholars stated that the conflict was significant in three respects: the first is that the war was seen by Japan as a way of acquiring colonies in Asia from other imperial countries; the second is that it was viewed by democratic countries as a war to protect the world from fascism; and the third is that it was seen by Asian peoples as a war of liberation. So, many Japanese scholars do not accept the theory of Hayashi Fusao which states that Japan freed Asia from European and American control.[1] Hashikawa Bunzo states that the slogan of the 'Greater East Asia Co-Prosperity Sphere' was an ideology which was created by the changes in relationships between the various countries in the world.[2] Fujiwara Akira states that Japan invaded South-East Asia to obtain military materials and to win the Sino-Japanese war.[3] And Imakawa Eiichi states that World War II did not solve the problems experienced by Asia since the 1920s: for example, economic systems are still controlled by the former colonial powers.[4]

On the other hand, scholars do not necessarily assess the role of the Japanese military occupation in South-East Asia. Some argue that Japanese soldiers trained many nationalists who fought against the European and American troops. For example, Ota Koki states that Japan taught the young leaders, students who went to Japan, and soldiers in the Philippines how to fight so as to secure their independence.[5] And Akashi Yoji says that Japan encouraged national liberation in South-East Asia.[6]

I would argue that Japan helped pro-Japanese peoples only. Overseas Chinese were treated very cruelly because almost all of them were pro-Chinese. Native peoples in South-East Asia could not obtain basic commodities during the Japanese occupation and many fell ill and died. Therefore, many of them hated Japan by the end of the war. The nature of these problems in Singapore will be examined later in this paper.

II: JAPANESE MILITARY PLANS FOR SOUTH-EAST ASIA BEFORE THE PACIFIC WAR

Japan had no plans to liberate South-East Asia. Japan did not plan for Singapore's independence during World War II. In August 1936 the Japanese government decided on a basic principle of southward expansion. This is called *Kokusaku no Kijun* or Fundamentals of National Policy. The judgement of the Tokyo trial in 1948 stated that this document proved Japan's ambition to control the world. Indeed, this document insisted on increasing military power to take account of future world conflict but it contained no concrete proposals for conquering the whole world.[7] In July 1940, because Germany attacked the European countries possessing colonies in South-East Asia, the *Daihonei Seifu Renraku Kaigi* or Imperial Headquarters-Cabinet Liaison Conference issued *Sekai Josei no Suii ni Tomonau Jikyoku-Shori Yoko* or Main Principles for Coping with the Changing World Situation, in order to conquer South-East Asia with military power if she had the chance to do so. But it included no plan for South-East Asian independence.[8]

In the same year the Japanese government issued a document called *Nichi Doku I Sujiku Kyoka ni Kansuru Ken* or the Document of Strengthening Relations among the Axis. This presented no plan for Singapore's freedom but it said that Malaya, including Singapore, should become a Seizonken or Life Zone of Japan. This was similar to the German concept of *Lebensraum*. Japan wanted to make Singapore a Japanese territory.[9] In his memoirs Colonel Ishii Akiho, a staff officer in the Japanese army in South-East Asia, said that Japan intended to make Malaya a Japanese territory and to give Indonesia, including Sumatra, autonomy at the beginning of the Pacific war. But in the midst of the battle in Malaya, Japan changed her policy: it was decided to make Sumatra a Japanese territory, too.[10]

In November 1941 an Imperial Headquarters-Cabinet Liaison Conference decided on *Nampo Senryochi Gyosei Jishi Yoryo* or Main Principles for Occupied Areas in South-East Asia and *Daihonei Rikugunbu* or Imperial Headquarters decided on the *Nampo sakusen ni Tomonau Senryochi Tochi Yoko* or Main Principles for Occupied Areas following the southward operations. These documents emphasised that restoration of public peace, acquisition of military materials and support for the military government were the most important aims during the war.[11] Before the Pacific war began on 8 December 1941 (December 7 in the USA), Japan had no plan to liberate South-East Asia but did possess a plan to make Singapore a territory.

After Japan occupied South-East Asia, Japan's fundamental policy regarding South-East Asia was the same as before. In May 1943 *Gozen Kaigi* or a conference with the Emperor decided that Malaya, Sumatra, Java, Borneo and Celebes would be Japanese territories and would supply sources of military materials. This decision was called *Daitoa Seiryaku Shido Taiko* or Main Principles for Operating the Greater East Asia Co-Prosperity Sphere.[12]

III: OVERSEAS CHINESE IN SINGAPORE

In 1940 there were about 590,000 overseas Chinese in Singapore or about 77.8 per cent of the population. [13] They engaged in almost all business and industry, for example mining, agriculture, commerce, transport, engineering works and so on.[14] Singapore was the centre of economic activity in South-East Asia, so overseas Chinese in Singapore played an important role in that activity. Japan knew this and wanted to use them for economic purposes during occupation.[15] But Singapore was also the base of the pro-Chinese movement of overseas Chinese in South-East Asia.[16] Therefore, there were some in the military who believed that Japan had to drive away overseas Chinese from Singapore. Before Japan invaded Singapore, she felt she had two alternatives, one was using overseas Chinese economic power, the other driving them away from there. When Japan occupied Singapore overseas Chinese were 'examined;' Japan was determined to utilise Chinese as directed so as to make amends for the support extended to Chiang Kai-shek by overseas Chinese.[17] Chinese merchants were ordered to sell Japanese food, clothing and other goods at low prices.

As soon as Japan occupied Singapore, overseas Chinese were punished for the crime of pro-Chinese activity. However, the Japanese were unable to discover who was pro-Chinese, so many innocent people were killed by Japanese soldiers on the coast of Changi, Tanahmerah and Punggol and offshore on Blakang Mati island in Singapore. It is said that between 40,000 and 70,000 people were killed in these 'examinations.'[18] After these 'examinations' overseas Chinese in Singapore and Malaya were forced to collect and pay 50 million dollars. Of this Singapore, which was renamed Shonan during the occupation, was forced to pay Japan 10 million dollars. Takase Toru, the civilian secretary of the general staff of the 25th army, threatened that he would not protect the lives of overseas Chinese if they did not pay the 50 million dollars.[19] Because of this terrible treatment, overseas Chinese in Singapore hated the military occupation.

The worst part of the treatment of overseas Chinese was the selling of opiates by Japan. Supplied by the British, there were many opiate users in South-East Asia. In the 1930s there were about 460,000. In Malaya 2.4 per cent of the population were opiate users; the problem was especially bad.[20] After Japan occupied Singapore, the Japanese military government took over the sale of opiates hoping to keep the opposition weak. Japan also wanted to obtain income from the sale of opiates so as to support military operations. In 1942 income from the sale of opiates in Singapore was about 50 per cent of the total income of the 25th army. The military government in Singapore depended significantly on the opiate income.[21] This shows that the Japanese army was anything but 'the Salvation Army' for overseas Chinese in South-East Asia.

IV: POLICY TOWARDS THE MALAYS

Because Japan needed the cooperation of Malays to establish the Greater East Asia Co-Prosperity Sphere, the intention was to use the sultans and the Islamic religion in order to control the Malays. So Japan treated them more gently than the Chinese. The Malays were seldom killed, unlike the Chinese. But Japan took away the authority and land of the sultans, forced them to obey the Emperor and to pray to gods in Japan at Shonan Jinja, a Shinto shrine. Akashi Yoji says, 'One of the important problems for the Japanese Military in the administration of occupied Malaya was the treatment of sultans and of the Islamic religion.'[22]

In March 1941 the first bureau of the army general staff drew up the Principles of Administration of Occupied Southern Areas. According to this plan, 'Malaya is to be placed under Japanese rule as part of the Japanese Empire and Malay states are to be guided by a supervisory military administration.'[23] Japan treated the Malays gently in order to control them as desired. And the Malays generally did not resist the Japanese. Japan gave the Malays education. For example, schools were built, language and religion taught, and an attempt was made to inspire in them the spirit of Japan. Japan especially trained them how to be good members and soldiers of the Co-Prosperity Sphere. Excellent students were sent to Japan to study more specialised fields. One of them, Wan Abdul Humid, became the director of the state of Pernas, and another, Ungku Abdul Aziz, the chancellor of the University of Malaysia. They have expressed their gratitude for their Japanese education during the war. But it should be understood that this education was given to make the Malays good members of the Co-Prosperity Sphere. Japan intended to make them middle class officials who would serve in the administration governed by the Emperor.[24]

The varying treatment between the Malays and the Chinese caused an important problem. Many anti-Japanese people were Chinese. So Japan wanted to catch and kill them. On the other hand, Japan made the Malays policemen and used them to catch the Chinese. The relationship between the Malays and the Chinese deteriorated. After World War II conflicts between the two peoples deepened. One of the origins of this problem is the different treatment of the two peoples under Japanese occupation.[25]

V: POLICY TOWARDS THE INDIAN SOLDIERS

Prior to the start of the Pacific war, the British army in Malaya included many Indian soldiers. Before the Japanese army went southward towards Singapore, it organised F. Kikan, led by Major Fujiwara Iwaichi. F. Kikan was the special group for operating the anti-British movement.

F. Kikan tried to persuade the Indian army in Malaya to join with the Japanese army and to fight against Britain to obtain Indian independence. F. Kikan succeeded in making a contract with the Indian Independence League (I.I.L.) led by Amar Singh and Pritam Singh, and the two promised to cooperate in establishing the Greater East Asia Co-Prosperity Sphere. F. Kikan intended to sweep the British army from the Malay peninsula and to capture Singapore. The I.I.L. wanted India to declare its independence. There were some differences in the goals of F. Kikan and I.I.L. These continued until the end of the war.

In December 1941 Mohan Singh, a captain in the Indian army, and his soldiers surrendered to the Japanese army; Mohan Singh joined with F. Kikan and organised the Indian National Army (I.N.A.) with the Indian prisoners of war. When the Japanese army arrived at Singapore, there were about 65,000 Indian prisoners of war. Some of them joined the I.N.A.; the others were sent to Rabaul and Timor island to work for Japan.[26]

In March 1942 F. Kikan was reorganised as Iwakuro Kikan, led by Colonel Iwakuro Hideo. Iwakuro Kikan strengthened the military power of the I.N.A., and gathered the Indian political refugees in Asia who tried to make India independent from Britain, for example, Rash Behari Bose in Japan. In April 1943 Iwakuro Kikan became Hikari Kikan led by Colonel Yamamoto Toshi. Hikari Kikan promoted Indian independence, too. It made Subhas Chanda Bose the president of the I.I.L. In October 1943 Chandra Bose created the Provisional Government of India in Singapore, and declared war on Britain.[27] F. Kikan, Iwakuro Kikan and Hikari Kikan all stated Japan would free India from Britain, and intended to use Indian military power. However, the I.N.A. had poor armaments with which to oppose the allied powers, and little connection with the independence movement in the motherland of India. The I.N.A. desired the independence of India.[28] But Japan could not always assist it because the real aim of Japan was pulling apart the Indian troops from the British army in South-East Asia.

VI: ORDINARY PEOPLES' LIVES

After Japan began to invade South-East Asia and to sweep the European and American military powers out, it had to manage the economy instead of the European countries and America. But Japan could not manage it alone. Before the war there was a triangular trade relationship between South-East Asia, Europe and the United States. All was now transformed. During the war Japan could not export food and other basic necessities to South-East Asia because Japan's shipping had been sunk by the allies and Japan had no agricultural and industrial surplus. Japan could not construct the 'Co-Prosperity Sphere.'[29] Japan concentrated its attention on obtaining military materials but not on supplying commodities for the peoples there. Prices of commodities rose day by day. When Japan was defeated, a price index in Shonan was about 350 times its pre-war level. Ordinary people could not afford the commodities, especially food and medicine.[30]

The ordinary people in Shonan were always hungry or sick and some died from lack of food and medicine. Shonan depended on rice imported from other places in South-East Asia. There was less rice each year: for example, 10,500 tons were imported between October 1942 and March 1943; 5,250 tons from October 1944 to March 1945.[31] Much of this rice was given to Japanese soldiers and to those who supported Japan. People in Singapore describe the period of the Japanese occupation as the 'Tapioca Age,' because tapioca was always eaten instead of rice.

CONCLUSION

After World War II many countries in South-East Asia were freed from European and American control, so the Japanese invasion can be regarded as fighting to achieve Asian independence. This view is suspect because many peoples in Asia had to fight against the colonial powers and had to solve problems themselves following Japan's defeat. For example, in Vietnam fighting continued until 1975 and in Singapore racial conflict broke out. In Singapore the Chinese wanted to build their own nation in order to defend themselves against invaders like Japan. Lee Kuan Yew, the prime minister of Singapore, said: 'My colleagues and I are of that generation of young men who went through the Second World War and the Japanese occupation and became determined that no one - neither the Japanese nor the British - had the right to push and kick us around. We were determined that we could govern ourselves and bring up our children in a country where we can be a self-respecting people.'[33] Chua Ser Koon, a scholar of the Japanese occupation, states that the freedom of Singapore did not come from the Japanese fighting against the British, but from the Japanese invasion and its harsh occupation.[34] It is important for Japanese scholars to appreciate how the Chinese who lived in Singapore regard the Japanese occupation because the extent of their suffering must be understood.

NOTES

1. Hayashi Fusao, *Daitoa Senso Kotei Ron*, Chuo Koron 1964. For a discussion of this, see: Ienaga Saburo, *Taiheiyou Senso*, Iwanami Shoten 1968, p. 9.
2. Hashikawa Bunzo, 'Toa Shin Chitsujo no Shinwa' *Kindai Nihon Seiji Shiso Shi II*, Yuhikaku 1970, p. 364.
3. Fuziwara Akira, *Taiheiyou Senso*, Buneido 1970, pp. 169-170.
4. Imakawa Eiichi, *Tonan Ajia Gendai Shi*, Aki Shobo 1972, p. 226.
5. Ota Koki, 'Nampo Gunsei no Tenkai to Tokushitsu' *Showa Shi no Gunbu to Seiji 4*, Daiichi Houki 1983, p. 74.
6. Akashi Yoji, 'The Koa Kunrenjo and Nampo Tokubetu Ryugakusei' *Shakai Kagaku Tokyu* 23.3.(1968) p. 576.
7. Gaimusho, *Nihon Gaiko Nempyo narabi Shuyo Bunsho 1840-1945*, Hara Shobo 1965, pp. 344-345.
8. *Ibid.*, pp. 437-438.
9. *Ibid.*, pp. 448-452.
10. Ishii Akiho, 'Nampo Gunsei Nikki' Boeicho Boei-Kenkyujo Senshibu, *Nampo no Gunsei*, Asagumo Shinbunsha 1985, p. 449.
11. Boeicho Boei-Kenkyujo Senshibu, *Nampo no Gunsei*, pp. 91-95.
12. Gaimusho, pp. 583-584.

13. Nomura Teikiti, *Singaporu to Marai Hanto*, Hounsha 1941, p. 80.
14. *Nanyo no Kakyo*, Nanyo Kyokai 1940, pp. 47-54.
15. *Kakyo Taisaku Shiken*, Taiheiyo Kyokai Chosa-Kyoku, pp. 1-14.
16. *Nanyo Kakyo Konichi Kyukoku Undo no Kenkyu*, Toa Kenkyujo: reprint Ryukei Shosya 1978.
17. Otabe Yuji, *Tokugawa Yoshichika no Jugonen Senso*, Aoki Shoten 1988, pp. 131-138.
18. Shu Yun Tsiao & Chua Ser Koon, *Nihon Gun Senryo Ka no Singaporu*, Aoki Shoten 1986.
19. Akashi Yoji, 'Japanese Policy Towards the Malayan Chinese 1941-1945' *Journal of Southeast Asian Studies*, 1-2 1970, pp. 70-75.
20. Nampo Kaihatu Kinko Chosa-Ka, 'Kyoei Ken no Ahen Jijo' *Zoku Gendai Shi Shiryo 12*, Misuzu Shobo 1986, pp. 193-207.
21. Otabe, pp. 138-141.
22. Akashi Yoji, 'Japanese Military Administration in Malaya' *Asian Studies* 7-1 1960, p. 81.
23. *Ibid.*, p. 82.
24. Otabe, pp. 156-159.
25. Matui Yayori, *Tamashii ni Hureru Ajia*, Asahi Shinbunsha 1985, pp. 159-166.
26. Maruyama Shizuo, *Indo Kokumin Gun*, Iwanami Shoten 1985, pp. 46-56.
27. *Ibid.*, pp. 46-78.
28. Fujiwara Iwaichi, *F Kikan*, Shingaku Shuppan 1985, pp. 209-223.
29. Kobayashi Hideo, *Daitoua Kyoeiken no Keisei to Hokai*, Ocha no Mizu Shobo 1975.
30.. Iwatake Teruhiko, *Nampo Gunsei Ka no Keizai Shisaku*, Kyuko Shoten 1981, pp. 545-546.
31. *Ibid.*, p. 502.
32. Stephon Leong, 'Maraya ni okeru Nihon Gunsei' *Sekai Shi no naka no Nihon Senryo*, Nihon Hyoron Sha 1985, p. 46.
33. Quoted in, Ishiwara Nobuo & Masuo Keizo, *Gaikoku no Kyokasho no naka no Nihon to Nihonjin*, Ikkou Sha 1988, p. 167.
34. Chua Ser Koon, 'The Chinese in Malaysia during the war' Lim Chool Kwa, ed., *The history of Chinese in Malaysia*, Persekutua Persatuan-Persatuan-Persatuan Siswazah-siswazah Universiti Taiwan Malaysia 1984.

Great Britain and the Japanese Peace Treaty, 1951

PETER LOWE

The British government long desired an early peace treaty with Japan, wavering only briefly in March 1951. Considerable frustration was felt in London at the inability in Washington to determine the future relationship with Japan and at President Truman's reluctance to resolve bickering between the State Department and the Pentagon.

The outbreak of the Korean war complicated the situation. The temptation on the American side to postpone a peace settlement until the Korean conflict came to an end was appreciable, particularly for the military. The principal British diplomatic representative in Tokyo reported in March 1951 that prominent members of General MacArthur's 'court' wished to defer it, fuelling speculation that MacArthur himself shared this opinion.[1] From January 1951 the pace of events quickened as President Truman encouraged his special consultant, John Foster Dulles, to proceed rapidly.[2] Dulles was extremely ambitious, ardently desiring a major role in formulation of foreign policy in the next administration. Dulles was prepared to use a whole array of tactics to deal with those who created difficulties - foreign governments, not least Great Britain, MacArthur before and after his dismissal, the right wing of the Republican party, the Japanese government and members of the administration in Washington. The Korean war rendered a settlement with Japan more urgent in Dulles's view, especially following Chinese intervention. It was essential that Japan should loyally support American efforts to block communism in East and South-East Asia.

The struggle in Korea gave rise to serious tension in Anglo-American relations. British policy-makers did not want to see the war escalating into full-scale conflict with China, still less into a third world war. American policy struck them as erratic, unpredictable and adventurous; they regarded their task as one of checking the more dangerous manifestations. To the Americans, British policy seemed pusillanimous and carping. Numerous acrid exchanges occurred between 1950 and 1953.[3] In the context of the Japanese treaty arguments over Korea sharpened British awareness of American sensitivity and meant that reservations were not pressed as far as otherwise might have happened. At the same time divergences in approach were clear and sometimes sharp.

Less sympathy for Japan existed in Britain than in the United States. This appears paradoxical, since the Americans had borne the brunt of the war against Japan and a desire for harsh retribution might have been expected. Probably because of the overwhelming American dominance in the occupation American interest in punishing the

Japanese had diminished. In Britain recollections of savage treatment meted out to prisoners of war (POWs) and civilians were vivid. Such reactions were common in the dominions and colonial territories of the Pacific and South-East Asia. Within Britain the most vehement anxieties involved economic issues with particular reference to textiles, shipbuilding and potteries. Memories of Japanese competition before the war were real and fostered apprehension among manufacturers and trade unionists that firms could be forced out of business with consequent unemployment. A Labour government pledged to full employment and all too conscious of the poverty of the interwar years pondered Japanese recovery with suspicion. Within the Commonwealth Australia and New Zealand feared swift revival which could produce the menace of a militaristic Japan. The future relationship between Japan and China - the Communists or the Kuomintang - was a vexed matter provoking anguished deliberations.

Direction in the Foreign Office lacked vigour at the top owing to the physical decline of Ernest Bevin and his reluctance to relinquish the post as foreign secretary; eventually he resigned in March 1951.[4] Sir Oliver Franks, the ambassador in Washington, explained to American officials that matters had drifted in recent months but a more incisive approach would now be seen.[5] Franks's explanation was in part a diplomatic defence and his belief that more effective conduct of policy would be forthcoming was not borne out. The new foreign secretary, Herbert Morrison, was immensely experienced in domestic politics, having made his reputation as 'boss' of the London Labour party. His interest in foreign affairs was minimal and he accepted the post because he wanted to be prime minister. Morrison had long desired the Labour leadership and saw his tenure of the Foreign Office as an added argument within his extensive curriculum vitae.[6] He frequently showed an irritable, petulant air, although ultimately this was overtaken by greater optimism after the San Francisco conference.

The first few months of Anglo-American discussions in 1951 witnessed significant disagreements. On 2 January Bevin told the cabinet that it was unclear how the United States envisaged handling the treaty and that Australia and New Zealand advocated a restrictive treaty in order to contain a potential threat.[7] In initial discussions Dulles showed that he was focusing on defence problems and the necessity of providing reassurance in the Pacific. When he made clear that he was contemplating a regional defence pact which would exclude Britain, reactions were predictably critical.[8] Dulles was moving towards resolving the serious questions involving Japan's future foreign and defence policies through continued American presence in Japan, modest Japanese rearmament, and a relationship with Australia and New Zealand which would give the United States the decisive say without opposition from Britain. British leaders resented Dulles's strategy and this contributed to deteriorating relations early in 1951.[9] At the end of February Dulles informed Franks that differences with Britain mainly involved Japanese shipbuilding capacity, restoration of allied property in Japan and a war guilt clause. Dulles was vigorously opposed to an attempt to cut shipbuilding capacity because any Japanese government trying to implement such a policy could not survive. He stated that he had an open mind over allied property, although MacArthur was hostile to compensating owners of property. Originally the British favoured inclusion of a war guilt clause but Dulles was deeply influenced by his experience in dealing with the Versailles treaty after the Great War and was firmly against inclusion. Franks told Dulles that this should not prove an insuperable problem.[10] He had modified his views over a defence pact away from an 'island chain' concept towards a triple agreement comprising the United States, Australia and New Zealand.

Pressures from British industries for imposing restrictions on Japanese industries were considerable. Textile interests had been vocal for some years. Sir Raymond Streat, chairman of the Cotton Board, conducted frequent discussions within the industry, with government, and in Tokyo (where he met MacArthur); Streat sought to achieve a realistic reaction based on tackling various defects within the industry while ensuring, through agreements with the Japanese textile industry, that competition did not assume dangerous proportions.[11] British anxiety was conveyed to Dulles who deemed it exaggerated. The textile lobby was the most vociferous in Britain and reflected attitudes within Lancashire. It was impossible to refer directly to textiles within the treaty. The chief British achievement was to ensure that Japan forfeited most favoured nation terms within the context of the Congo Basin treaties.[12] The outcome was that Japanese textile competition in Africa was reduced. The government was more worried over shipbuilding than textiles. This was because shipbuilding fused economic and strategic aspects. The potteries of Staffordshire evoked less concern in Whitehall but the two MPs for Stoke-on-Trent were vocal in underlining fears in the pottery towns.[13]

The most difficult stage in Anglo-American discussions occurred in March and April. Shortly after taking over as foreign secretary Morrison chaired a cabinet meeting, in Attlee's absence, on 22 March. He emphasised two related problems which were of political rather than economic character. He stated that the Chinese Communist government must participate in the negotiations leading to a treaty; over Taiwan he proposed that Japanese sovereignty should be relinquished formally to 'China' without prejudice to a decision as to which Chinese authority should possess Taiwan.[14] This reminded those present of recent acrimonious exchanges with the United States over a possible compromise aimed at ending the Korean war and over the arguments surrounding condemnation of China for aggression in Korea. The likelihood of further rows resulting from American hatred of Chinese communism led cabinet members to consider the wisdom of delaying a treaty. To proceed immediately could involve American pressure in support of Kuomintang participation. The Commonwealth was not in agreement on how best to advance and problems existed because of the continuance of the war in Korea. The cabinet 'invited the Foreign Secretary to seek means of delaying further proceedings for the discussion of a Japanese Peace Treaty.'[15]

The emerging difficulties disturbed Dulles who referred critically to the negative or vacillating views in London during meetings in April. Oliver Franks assured Dean Acheson that there were no insuperable obstacles precluding cooperation regarding a treaty. Franks confirmed this to Dulles on 5 April who nevertheless expressed his doubts, 'We were beginning to wonder whether or not the United Kingdom still adhered to their previous desire for conclusion of an early Treaty.'[16] The British attitude over China and Taiwan rendered progress extremely difficult and delays had occurred while ascertaining British views towards defence arrangements for Pacific security. Franks reminded Dulles of the controversies caused by 'MacArthuritis' - 'He pointed out that whether one agreed or disagreed with what General MacArthur was doing, it was, nevertheless, a fact that his actions had caused considerable concern in Europe and Britain, and that that conditioned to some degree United Kingdom actions.'[17] A few weeks later Dulles remarked, at a meeting with American defence chiefs, that, 'it was not yet apparent whether the British really wanted to go along with us or whether they wanted to split with us on Japan as they had on China.'[18]

The Foreign Office immediately recognised the error in vacillating over Britain's commitment to a treaty and, at Morrison's prompting, the cabinet reversed its position when it met on 2 April. Morrison emphasised that the Americans were keen to advance and that Japan was critical of Britain for wishing to delay. This threatened to undermine British credibility and it was agreed that Britain should resume discussions. It was noted that the Soviet Union should be permitted an opportunity to participate in talks concerning a treaty.[19] Work in formulating draft treaties had proceeded in Washington and London. An American provisional draft was submitted but was regarded as too simple and amateurish in the Foreign Office. C. H. Johnston and the Japan and Pacific department, aided by G. C. Fitzmaurice, the chief legal adviser, produced a draft in March which was approved by other government departments and by other parts of the Foreign Office. As Roger Makins minuted on 5 April, it was regrettable that the British draft could not have been devised before the American draft.[20] The permanent under-secretary, Sir William Strang, observed patronisingly that: 'The Americans will probably not take kindly to this accurate draft of ours. May prefer their own rather slapdash productions. But we must try it on, even though we are rather late with it.'[21] Morrison grumbled that the papers were very lengthy and had reached him in a box at a function he had attended that night - 'it is now past 11 p.m. & I must get my week-end sleep to make up for the 3 a.m.s of the week. Mr Barclay asks for return a.m. tomorrow. Well, I don't propose to lose my sleep & my health because of that. So here are the pp. I have "looked" at & as he suggested - in view of its length this is all that is poss[ible]... So I accept assurances that the great bulk has Cab[inet] authority & I note that HMG & the Commonwealth not committed. On this basis transmission can proceed. But don't forget Cab[inet] at right time.'[22]

Detailed discussions took place in Washington during April and

Franks reported broad satisfaction. On 4 May he stated in a telegram that the talks had reduced but not eliminated the area of disagreement on the substance of a treaty. Significant disagreements remained, notably over China and Taiwan, but understanding had been obtained regarding procedure and each side possessed a better appreciation of the differences between them.[23] Dulles visited London in early June and engaged in comprehensive exchanges with British ministers which did more to fulfil Franks's wish for a fuller mutual understanding. On 5 June Kenneth Younger, the minister of state in the Foreign Office, chaired a meeting in the House of Commons attended by British and American officials. Younger summarised disagreement over China and proposed a formula originated by Canada: neither the Peking nor Taiwan governments should sign a treaty and reference to 'China' should be vague and should allow for adherence at a later date. It would be difficult for Britain to sign a treaty also signed by Chiang Kai-shek's government. Dulles responded that the intention was to persuade maximum possible adherence to the treaty by the nations involved. It was essential to produce a treaty which would be ratified by the American Senate. He denied a report in *The Times* that he had arrived in London with the aim of securing concurrence in Kuomintang adherence. Dulles commented on alternative formulae. It might be feasible to apply a treaty to China without providing for signature on behalf of China; a series of bilateral treaties should be concluded in place of a multilateral one; or it might be possible to allow governments from the principal parties to adhere to a multilateral agreement before or after ratification which would enable the Japanese government to determine recognition for purposes of a peace treaty. Dulles stressed that, 'He was above all anxious to keep the Japanese Peace Treaty free from entanglement with the Chinese problem....'[24]

As regards Taiwan, Dulles said its status should not be changed by a treaty apart from terminating Japanese rights. On the defence question Dulles stated that the United States was securing military facilities in Japan and he believed that if the details were known in Britain then alarm over future Japanese bellicosity would vanish. Because it was a sensitive matter in Japan little could be said at present. In further exchanges on 6 June divergent opinions regarding China were more marked and Dulles rejected the British preference for leaving a decision on Chinese accession to a group of the principal parties commanding a majority for recognising either Peking or Taiwan. Younger observed that once a treaty had been signed Japan would be free to decide itself. While correct in a formal sense, this underestimated the pressure that could be brought to bear by the United States.[25]

At a subsequent meeting on 6 June Morrison referred to potent expressions of sympathy for former POWs conveyed in the House of Commons. Care must be exercised in considering Japanese rearmament. He would have preferred a written statement of assurance concerning Japanese rearmament, although he appreciated the position of the Japanese government. He would accept the substance of an assurance. Dulles replied frankly that the only permanent guarantee against future

Japanese militarism was an indefinite extension of the occupation. His solution was that: 'The United States Government wanted to continue with the substance of the occupation but not the form. They wanted to maintain United States armed forces in Japan with the consent of the Japanese.'[26] In order to satisfy all interests a realistic solution to defence issues had to be reconciled with Japanese sovereignty. If a treaty was too emphatic in restricting Japanese rearmament it would not be acceptable to the Japanese people. Morrison commented that assistance to former POWs would best be handled by a body such as the Red Cross rather than by the state. On China Dulles reiterated the view that each Chinese government should sign but Morrison replied that any arrangement whereby Chiang Kai-shek's government signed would be condemned in Britain. On Taiwan Dulles stated that this should be left to the United Nations to decide and Morrison thought that there was much to be said in favour of this approach. Morrison indicated British fears over shipping for both strategic and economic reasons.

Dulles met the Chancellor of the Exchequer, Hugh Gaitskell, on 6 June. Gaitskell stated that while the Japanese desire for a liberal treaty was understood it had to be realised that there was a strong anti-Japanese feeling in Britain. This was inspired primarily by Japanese treatment of POWs. Public opinion would resent Japan escaping leniently with far smaller reparations payments than Germany had done. Dulles drew attention to the American burden in sustaining the Japanese economy throughout the occupation but they had refrained from utilising Japanese gold deposits so that Japan would possess resources upon regaining independence. However, if the gold could be distributed among the allies the United States would claim priority so that the 2,000 million US dollars advanced to Japan would be reimbursed. In comparing Japan with Germany Dulles underlined the loss of the Japanese colonial empire - 'He claimed that no nation had ever paid such a severe penalty for a war of aggression.'[27] Gaitskell maintained that a distinction had to be made between what was forfeited by a country vanquished in war and what was gained by the victors. Comparison with Germany was not satisfactory owing to the division of the country. The difference on reparations was manifest. Gaitskell revealed his animus against Japan in remarking that it would be preferable for the United States to take all of the gold instead of returning it to Japan. Dulles reminded him of the importance of raising living standards in Japan.

On 8 June Dulles met the president of the Board of Trade, Sir Hartley Shawcross. British concern over the Congo Basin treaties was conveyed: there was no wish to exclude Japanese goods entirely from the areas involved but anxiety existed at the danger of an influx of large quantities of cheap Japanese textiles. The British balance of payments must be watched: as a result of the rearmament drive textile exports were designated to rise by 40 per cent over the 1950 figure. Apprehension at Japanese competition was a major political factor in Britain.[28] Dulles referred to Italy as a basis for comparison for the Congo Basin treaties:

the decision had been made not to remove Italian rights under the Saint-Germain convention, although it had been modified. The United States envisaged the same procedure applying to Japan. Shawcross rejected comparison with Italy because it had held colonies in Africa and did not have the low labour standards of Japan. He was shortly to receive a delegation of Conservative MPs from Lancashire alarmed at Japanese competition.

It became clear during Dulles's visit that while he would take serious note of British representations, he was determined to complete negotiations reasonably quickly. Sir Esler Dening observed on 7 June that Dulles had emphasised to Younger that the London talks could lead to great success or great failure. The repercussions for Anglo-American and for Anglo-Japanese relations would be grave if agreement could not be reached. Some progress had been made on rearmament, the position of China and Taiwan. There appeared to be a prospect of American concessions regarding assets in neutral countries and it would be sensible to accept this in the light of American refusal to modify their attitude over Japanese gold.[29]

Morrison and Dulles resumed consideration of Chinese aspects on 8 June. Morrison expressed British preference for a multilateral treaty rather than a series of bilateral treaties. Britain did not want either the Peking government or that in Taiwan to emerge favourably and was willing to accept Dulles's proposal that neither the Communist nor the Kuomintang government should be eligible under the formula without the approval of, let it be suggested, two-thirds of the principal parties signing a treaty.[30] Dulles was preoccupied with restoring Japanese sovereignty. The Japanese government would have to reach its own decisions. He regarded it as inconceivable that Japan would conclude a treaty with Taiwan as though the latter could commit the whole of China. Personally he would welcome Japanese arrangements with the Communist government in Peking to handle certain matters. Dulles spoke of the generous concession he had made: when the British opposed his proposal he had accepted the British one which attained the limit, and perhaps more than the limit, of what was politically feasible in the United States. If the Truman administration succeeded in persuading the Senate to accept this solution it would be explicable mainly in terms of Dulles's own influence within the Republican party. The issue was extremely delicate and required meticulous handling. No doubt he exaggerated for his own reasons but there was much validity in his comments, given the vehement views expressed by Senators Taft, McCarthy and others.

The Foreign Office was broadly satisfied with the outcome of Dulles's visit. When Morrison had introduced the subject in cabinet on 28 May some members were less enthusiastic. He reminded them that they could opt either for a relatively liberal or restrictive treaty. Bearing in mind past cabinet deliberations, the international situation, the state of Anglo-American relations, the importance of reconciliation with Japan and of defeating communism, and of opinions within the Commonwealth, Morrison believed the more liberal approach should be endorsed. Some of his colleagues expressed doubts, especially regarding Japanese rearmament; it is likely that Gaitskell was among them but the cabinet minutes do not identify individuals.[31] Morrison reported subsequently and the cabinet approved his conduct of the talks. Thus the position on the central issues in mid-June 1951 was that neither Chinese government would be invited to sign and that the treaty would allow for Japan's concluding a bilateral treaty of peace on the same, or substantially the same, terms as in the treaty itself; the Japanese government would be free to recognise the Peking government if it wished to do so. The public announcement would state that no attempt would be made to prejudge the future of Taiwan or the Pescadores. With reparations it was agreed that gold would not be referred to directly in the treaty; reference would be included to Japan's obligation to pay reparations. Japanese assets in neutral or former enemy countries should be handed to the Red Cross to be utilised in assisting former POWs. Dulles had accepted the British contention concerning the Congo Basin treaties.

One important qualification in the economic sphere involved shipping: the British preference was for unqualified national treatment on the basis of reciprocity pending conclusion of bilateral trade treaties while the United States wanted this qualified by a 'let-out' clause alluding to the necessity of safeguarding balance of payments. The Foreign Office's conclusion was that the talks had achieved the best compromise attainable - 'We have had to sacrifice our view on disposal of gold and Americans have had to sacrifice theirs on Chinese Nationalist participation.'[32] Morrison assented to a request from Acheson and Dulles that the public statement agreed upon in London should not be issued in that form for domestic reasons in the United States.[33]

Dulles proposed that the United States and Britain should prepare a joint draft treaty. This was warmly welcomed in London since it afforded a better means of influencing the final treaty. Dulles's motive was probably a combination of offering something to placate the British while ensuring that he retained the decisive voice. The contribution made by British officials to the drafting process, particularly that of Fitzmaurice, was important but was not given adequate acknowledgement in Washington. Herbert Morrison expressed annoyance at the beginning of August that the Americans were taking all the credit for drafting. A telegram was sent to Washington on 7 August protesting and urging an amendment in American tactics:

> We do not wish to advertise the influence we have exerted behind the scenes but in the circumstances...we think that excessive modesty about our contribution would be against the interests of His Majesty's Government and of Anglo-United States cooperation generally. It seems to us that it would also be to the United States Government's own advantage in their relations with the other Governments concerned to avoid letting the draft Treaty appear as a purely single-handed American achievement.[34]

The embassy in Washington replied that Dulles had alluded to British assistance but that the press had given this aspect little emphasis. Franks believed that Britain had benefited from the impression sometimes conveyed that the United States was dragging a reactionary Britain along more progressive paths. It was suspected that Dulles personally may have inspired some reports. The decision of the Soviet Union to participate in the San Francisco conference was likely to encourage more attention on Britain's part as co-sponsor of the conference.[35] Certainly from the viewpoint of presenting matters in such a way as to appeal to right-wing Republicans, Franks was correct and Dulles's strategy was vindicated.

Reaction in Britain to publication of the treaty ranged from congratulatory to resigned or critical. The Textile Firms Advisory Committee had hosted a dinner on 3 July at which government representatives were given a pessimistic assessment of the likely development of the British industry because of growing Japanese competition. They anticipated severe competition but agreed that the peace treaty could not in itself prevent competition; but they held that constant and close contact with Japanese manufacturers should help in persuading the Japanese of the undesirability of cut-throat competition; and they hoped that the British government would be willing to make representations warning against reversion to pre-war trade practices.[36] Morrison kept this in mind and spoke firmly to Yoshida Shigeru, the Japanese prime minister, at the San Francisco conference.[37] Various MPs raised queries in the Commons on 4 July concerning textiles, potteries and other industries.[38] The chief Conservative spokesman on foreign affairs, Anthony Eden, gently questioned the procedure followed in negotiating the treaty with particular reference to the Commonwealth when he spoke on 12 July: it would have been preferable had Britain and the Commonwealth agreed on a draft treaty before circulation of a treaty. It would now be discussed without full knowledge of the views held within the Commonwealth. Morrison conceded that the procedure was not customary but defended it on the grounds that the whole situation regarding the treaty was unusual.[39]

The government was most concerned over shipbuilding. C. H. Johnston reviewed the position in late August.[40] He recalled that a decision had been taken in April that shipbuilding should not figure directly in the treaty and that efforts to obtain a reduction in Japanese shipbuilding capacity should be made outside a peace treaty. The Japanese government maintained that capacity did not exceed needs. Capacity was given as 810,100 gross tons a year in 1945 but because of effective suspension of shipbuilding Japan's capacity in July 1951 was 676,000 gross tons a year. Japanese yards were functioning at between 70 per cent and 80 per cent with output between 400,000 and 500,000 gross tons a year. By the end of 1952 Japan would possess 1,549,000 tons of ocean-going ships. A larger fleet would be required to facilitate trade with the United States and other countries so as to compensate for the loss of China. An increase of 700,000 tons by 1953 would come from new construction and requirements in 1956 were estimated at 2,956,000 tons of ocean-going shipping with 820,000 tons of coastal shipping; these figures assumed that Japanese ships would carry around 50 per cent of Japan's overseas trade. Johnston remarked that estimation of Japanese foreign trade for 1956 was problematical; the Japanese statement did not allow for ships purchased in Japan in recent months. After 1956 the Japanese fleet would either continue to expand or Japanese competition for building orders would become intense.[41]

There appeared to be no economic argument for saying that Japanese shipbuilding capacity would be greater than approximately 400,000 tons a year. Britain contended that Japan should possess only as large a merchant marine as it could employ in fair competition with ships of other flags. Before the war Japan had discriminated against foreign shipping through subsidising shipbuilding. The British industry was concerned that the Japanese merchant marine should not expand unduly in the years following implementation of the peace treaty so as to save foreign exchange. Otherwise Japan might find itself possessing an uneconomic fleet which could operate only via discriminatory practices analogous to those applied before the war. Ministers decided on 30 July that the United States should be told that Japan's shipbuilding capacity was excessive and should be reduced. This view had been communicated to Washington on 14 August but no reply had yet been received.[42] Morrison told the cabinet on 1 August that the United States was disposed to accept Japanese arguments on shipbuilding. In his view there was no justification for Japan having capacity in excess of about 400,000 tons a year. The cabinet noted difficulties arising from Japanese competition in general and not simply in shipbuilding. The possibility of incorporating restrictive provisions in a peace treaty was again rejected and it was understood that the growth of population and the wisdom of encouraging a democratic system necessitated magnanimity. It was agreed that the United States should be pressed further and the cooperation of Australia and New Zealand enlisted: the southern dominions were, however, preoccupied with security rather than economic considerations.[43]

The conference in San Francisco assembled in early September amidst apprehension that the Soviet Union would cause difficulty. Dean Acheson chaired the opening session in masterly fashion; Andrei Gromyko, the principal Soviet spokesman, seemed to be going through the motions of protest rather than maneouvring with any serious hope of disrupting proceedings. Herbert Morrison agreed reluctantly, and under much pressure, to attend the conference at all.[44] He had arranged a holiday and stipulated that he would be present only for the concluding ceremonies. Attlee instructed Kenneth Younger to attend the opening session. Morrison did not appear to appreciate the irony of his previous complaint that the United States was dominating the treaty negotiations too heavily, which was compounded by his failure to be present for the entire conference. Yoshida Shigeru overcame his reluctance to attend and played an active role in San Francisco. He visited Younger on 3 September and expressed his gratitude for Britain's contribution to the treaty: it was 'more generous than I expected.'[45] Yoshida emotionally referred to the lengthy tradition of Anglo-Japanese amity sadly vitiated by the war. Japanese leaders before the Pacific war had, in Yoshida's words, gone 'crazy and lost common sense and he hoped this would never recur.'[46] Younger reported that the conference had opened encouragingly. Acheson was a tough chairman, if somewhat irregular. Gromyko spoke very rapidly and predictably in denouncing the treaty. His proposals and those of the Poles were swiftly voted down. Dulles and Younger made formal sponsoring speeches in the afternoon - 'I thought that Dulles's references to China were moderately phrased; listening to him, I could not help reflecting that the distance American thinking must move in regard to China was much less than the distance it had moved in the last six years in regard to Japan.'[47] The conference ended on 8 September on a placid note; the Soviet, Polish and Czech delegates did not attend. At Acheson's request Morrison inaugurated the formal signatures.[48]

George Clutton of the British liaison mission in Tokyo reported that the treaty had been welcomed in a restrained manner by the Japanese people. There were no spontaneous public displays and flags were not flown from public buildings. Newspapers published unanimous statements of gratitude and the people were urged to prepare for new responsibilities shortly to be faced.[49] When Clutton saw Yoshida on 19 September the prime minister informed him of the emperor's reactions. He had reminded Emperor Hirohito of the magnanimity of the treaty:

> The Emperor agreed that it was indeed a generous Treaty and to him unexpectedly generous. He then added, however, that it was for him a bitter blow that Japan should in the reign of the grandson of the Great Emperor Meiji have lost all her overseas possessions. Yoshida says that he told the Emperor that this was no time for murmurs of that sort.[50]

Clutton commented that undue significance should not be attached to the emperor's remarks. At the same time it was easy to forget that 'in its territorial clauses the Treaty is in fact Draconian and that the territorial losses it had imposed on Japan will be remembered by many Japanese for a long time.'[51]

Just before the close of the San Francisco conference Morrison spoke to Yoshida and emphasised that the Japanese government must follow progressive social and economic policies. He underlined the need for employers and trade unions to act responsibly. The specific causes for concern felt by British firms and trade unions were directly cited by Morrison:

> There was anxiety in Great Britain lest pre-war conditions of sweated labour and competition were revived. In the interests of the people of Japan and of relations between Japan and Britain it was essential that this should not happen. Indeed I felt that my signing of the Treaty would be justified only if the Japanese Government took steps to see that there was no recurrence of these conditions.[52]

Yoshida professed complete concurrence and said his policy was to democratise Japan. He raised the position of China and stated that there could be no stability while communism prevailed. Morrison said that Britain had no wish to dictate a Japanese decision regarding Chinese recognition. It was vital that the decision reached by the Japanese government should be carefully considered. Yoshida was unsurprisingly non-committal. The discussion ended with a brief exchange of thoughts regarding respective ambassadorial appointments consequent on the formal termination of the occupation. Morrison quaintly observed that a man with brains and energy should be appointed; given these qualities disagreements could be tolerated.[53]

The Chinese issue was the most delicate aspect and the one which created the greatest controversy in the short term. This was inevitable for whatever happened would have been controversial. These developments cannot be considered in detail here but the essential features require brief summary to round off discussion of the peace treaty. Dulles acted contrary to the agreement reached with Morrison in June in pressurising Yoshida to recognise Chiang Kai-shek's government. Given the continuation of the Korean war and the vitriolic attitudes toward China found within the Republican party, and bearing in mind Dulles's political aspirations, he had little choice but to act as he did. Reactions in London were bitter. A new Conservative government assumed office in October 1951 with Anthony Eden at the Foreign Office. Both Eden and Morrison condemned Dulles's conduct and deprecated the recognition accorded to the Kuomintang regime in Taiwan.

Finally, what did Britain contribute to the peace treaty and how effective was Anglo-American cooperation? The British role was more significant than has sometimes been argued but not as extensive as some have maintained.[54] Much of the actual drafting of the treaty was the work of British officials, notably Fitzmaurice.[55] The rather arrogant view of the Foreign Office that they were better at drafting treaties than the State Department was justified. However, it is misleading to focus too heavily on the drafting process. It is clear that the British would have adopted a more restrictive approach had it not been for American pressure. Britain originally contemplated a war guilt clause, imposing restrictions on shipbuilding, retention of gold and defining limits to Japanese rearmament. These were not pursued as a result of appreciating the strength of American opinion in favour of a liberal treaty. The cabinet reached its own decisions but within the framework established by the United States. Dulles wished to involve the British fully and would hardly have proposed a joint draft otherwise. But cooperation would culminate in what the Americans desired.

Compared with the recurring tensions in relations over Korea the negotiations over the San Francisco treaty were in general amicable. John Foster Dulles handled the whole topic with skill, flexibility and astuteness. The consequences of the treaty for Japan were more positive and long lasting than officials in the British Foreign Office forecast in the spring and summer of 1951.

NOTES

I am most grateful to the Nuffield Foundation for generously assisting the research for this paper through its Social Sciences Small Grants Scheme.

1. See letters from George Clutton to R. H. Scott, 19 and 31 March 1951, FJ FO 371/92537/211/G and 235, Public Record Office, Kew. Copyright material from the Public Record Office appears by permission of Her Majesty's Stationery Office. I wish to thank the staff of the Public Record Office for their assistance in the course of my research there.
2. Letter from Acheson to Marshall, 9 January 1951, enclosing memorandum to Truman, 9 January 1951, *Foreign Relations of the United States*, hereafter cited as *FRUS*, 1951 VI, part 1, 787-9.
3. For Anglo-American relations before and during the Korean war, see Peter Lowe, *The Origins of the Korean War* (London, 1986), 'Great Britain, the United Nations and the Korean War, 1950-3' in Ian Nish (ed.), *Aspects of the Korean War, International Studies* 1987/1 (London School of Economics, London, 1987), pp. 1-22, 'The Settlement of the Korean War,' in J. W. Young (ed.), *The Foreign Policy of Churchill's Peacetime Administration, 1951-1955* (Leicester, 1988), pp. 207-31. See also Rosemary Foot, *The Wrong War: American Policy and the Dimensions of the Korean Conflict, 1950-1953* (London and Ithaca, 1985) and C. A. MacDonald, *Korea: the War before Vietnam* (London, 1986).
4. For a discussion of Bevin's final phase, see Alan Bullock, *The Life and Times of Ernest Bevin* III *Foreign Secretary 1945-51* (London, 1983), pp. 743-835.
5. Memorandum by Allison, 5 April 1951, *FRUS* 1951 VI, part 1, 965-6.
6. For an account of Morrison's career, see Bernard Donoughue and G. W. Jones, *Herbert Morrison: Portrait of a Politician* (London, 1973).
7. Cabinet minutes, 2 January 1951, CM 1(51)4, Cab 128/19, Public Record Office.
8. Washington to FO, 12 January 1951 and FO to Washington, 23 January 1951, FO 371/92529/16/G.
9. FO to Tokyo, 30 January 1951, FO 371/92529/24/G.
10. Washington to FO, 28 February 1951, FO 371/92532/100.
11. For the economic and political views of the urbane Streat, see M. W. Dupree (ed.), *The Diaries of Sir Raymond Streat* 2 Vols. (Manchester, 1987), II, pp. 423-615 for the period, 1948-51.
12. For a summary of the complexities surrounding this aspect, see minute by C. H. Johnston, 5 May 1951, FO 371/92549/408.
13. See, for example, the questions and remarks by the two MPs for the Stoke-on-Trent divisions in the House of Commons, 4 July 1951, contained in FO 371/92562/671. The MPs were A. Edward Davies (Labour, Stoke-on-Trent, North) and Ellis Smith (Labour, Stoke-on-Trent, South).
14. Cabinet minutes, 22 March 1951, CM 22(51)3, Cab 128/19.
15. *Ibid.*
16. Memorandum by Allison, 5 April 1951, *FRUS* 1951, VI, part 1, 965.
17. *Ibid*, 966.
18. *Ibid*, p. 1020, memorandum by Dulles for Acheson, 25 April 1951.
19. Cabinet minutes, 2 April 1951, CM 23(51)7, Cab 128/19.
20. Minute by Makins, 5 April 1951, FO 371/92538/222. The British provisional draft extended to 37 pages when printed and was communicated to Washington on 23 March 1951.
21. Minute by Strang, 5 April 1951, *ibid.*
22. Minute by Morrison, 6 April 1951, *ibid.*
23. Washington to FO, 4 May 1951, FO 371/92547/366.
24. Record of meeting held at House of Commons, 5 June 1951, FO 371/92554/513.
25. Record of meeting, 6 June 1951, FO 371/92554/514.
26. Record of meeting at Foreign Office, 6 June 1951, FO 371/92554/515.
27. Treasury memorandum by A. J. Phelps, 6 June 1951, FO 371/92557/564A.
28. Record of meeting at House of Commons, 8 June 1951, FO 371/92554/516.
29. Minute by Dening, 7 June 1951, FO 371/92555/538.
30. Record of meeting held at Foreign Office, 8 June 1951, FO 371/92556/547.
31. Cabinet minutes, 28 May 1951, CM 37(51)7, Cab 128/19.
32. FO to Washington (two telegrams), 15 June 1951, FO 371/92555/539.
33. FO to Washington (two telegrams), 22 June 1951, *ibid.* 34. FO to Washington, 7 August 1951, FO 371/92585/1144.
35. Washington to FO, 21 August 1951, FO 371/92586/1168.
36. Minute by C. P. Scott, 8 July 1951, FO 371/92561/670.
37. San Francisco to FO, 12 September 1951, FO 371/92616/5.
38. Extracts from *Parliamentary Debates*, 4 July 1951, contained in FO 371/92562/671.
39. Extracts from *Parliamentary Debates*, 12 July 1951, contained in FO 371/92566/758.
40. Minute by C. H. Johnston, 28 August 1951, FO 371/92592/1309/G.
41. *Ibid.*
42. *Ibid.*
43. Cabinet minutes, 1 August 1951, CM 57(51)5, Cab 128/20.
44. See Washington to FO, 18 July 1951, FO 371/92568/777 where Acheson and Dulles were reported as strongly urging Morrison to attend. Morrison initially suggested that the date of formal signature

be changed to permit him to reach San Francisco on his return from a Norwegian cruise but this could not be fulfilled. Morrison then decided to arrive in San Francisco on the evening of 7 September on the assumption that he would deliver a speech the following day. See Washington to FO, 20 July 1951 and FO to Washington, 24 July 1951, FO 371/92570/810.

45. San Francisco to FO, 4 September 1951, FO 371/92594/1334.

46. *Ibid.*

47. San Francisco to FO, 6 September 1951, FO 371/92595/1354.

48. San Francisco to FO, 8 September 1951, FO 371/92595/1368.

49. Tokyo to FO, 13 September 1951, FO 371/92598/1392.

50. Letter from Clutton to R. H. Scott, 20 September 1951, FO 371/92599/1419.

51. *Ibid.*

52. San Francisco to FO, 12 September 1951, FO 371/92614/5.

53. *Ibid.*

54. For an account placing emphasis on American policy-making, see Chihiro Hosoya, 'The Road to San Francisco: the shaping of American policy on the Japanese Peace Treaty,' *The Japanese Journal of American Studies* I (1981), 87-117. For observations on the peace treaty in the light of British policy concerning the Cold War, see Ritchie Ovendale, 'Britain and the Cold War in Asia' in Ovendale (ed.), *The Foreign Policy of the British Labour Governments, 1945-1951* (Leicester, 1984), pp. 139-42.

55. Minute by R. H. Scott, 13 August 1951, recording a message of appreciation from Dulles for G. C. Fitzmaurice, FO 371/92583/1062.

Soviet-Japanese Normalisation and the Foreign Policy Ideas of the Hatoyama Group

TANAKA TAKAHIKO

I INTRODUCTION

On 19 October 1956 the Soviet Union and Japan issued a joint declaration, whereby diplomatic relations between the two countries were restored. Soviet-Japanese normalisation possesses considerable significance in the context of Japan's diplomatic history after 1945. Since the San Francisco peace treaty one of the most important goals of Japanese foreign policy had been to improve relations with the USSR because the latter had not been a party to the San Francisco treaty. Territorial problems regarding the disposal of the Kurils and southern Sakhalin could not be solved during the course of the normalisation talks in 1956. The two countries failed to solve the most controversial problems regarding the future of the Kurils. The mid-1950s saw a transformation of the cold war with an emerging trend of 'thaw' or detente. In 1953 the Korean war ended and in 1954 a temporary halt in the Indochina conflict occurred. In 1955 the Austrian State treaty was concluded and diplomatic relations between the Federal Republic of Germany and the Soviet Union were established. In the broader context of the mid-1950s Soviet-Japanese normalisation was an attempt to reduce international tension and to foster detente.

After the fall of the Yoshida government in December 1954 Hatoyama Ichiro, then president of the Democratic party, came into office. Shortly after the establishment of his administration, Soviet-Japanese normalisation was defined by Hatoyama as one of the most significant goals of his government. The Soviet Union was also willing to commence negotiations which started in London in June 1955. Hatoyama and his advisers pursued a most positive attitude towards the resumption of diplomatic relations with Moscow. Their efforts were hampered by domestic opponents but eventually Hatoyama visited Moscow and concluded the joint declaration by shelving the territorial questions. The aim of this paper is to explore the reasons why Hatoyama and his associates embarked upon this policy. Hatoyama was advised by prominent retired diplomats. The most important was Sugihara Arata. Another was Matsumoto Shunichi who was appointed as plenipotentiary for the negotiations: he had served as ambassador to Britain between 1952 and 1954. Hatoyama was deeply influenced by his advisers. Their views were determined by the evolving international situation and by their own perspective. Nationalism influenced Hatoyama: he wished to improve Japan's international status and enhance her independence.

II PERCEPTION OF THE INTERNATIONAL POLITICAL SITUATION IN THE MID-1950s

Their assessment of the Soviet Union had changed significantly after the death of Stalin. However, even before this, in 1952, Hatoyama made clear his desire for normalisation. As regards motivation he wrote in his memoirs as follows:

> In those days around 1952, I often read the following argument in certain American magazines: 'the most dangerous year will be 1952.' It was argued that war would be the most probable in the year because it would be the year when the US and the USSR would accomplish their full military power for the first time since World War II. This consideration made me anxious while I was under medical treatment after I had suffered from a cerebral haemorrhage. I thought that if war broke out between the US and the Soviet Union, Japan would be a battlefield and would be attacked by the Russians. This thought led me to conclude that Japan should restore normal diplomatic relations with Russia as soon as possible.[1]

Hatoyama maintained in his memoirs that his wish for normalisation was his own idea. Sugihara contended that Hatoyama's address in 1952 clearly reflected a memorandum he had submitted. This memorandum has not been located but Sugihara's memoirs contain an outline.[2]

Sugihara assumed that superpower rivalry was the decisive element in the international scene in the far east.[3] The dangers inherent in the Korean war seriously affected Japan's security. He wrote:

> Given the continuation of the state of war between Japan and the Soviet Union, the Russians were in the position where they could launch hostile activities against Japan without complying with a procedure, e.g. renewal of declaration of war on Japan.[4]

The continuation of the state of war with the USSR was expected to become sufficient justification, on the Russian part, for a surprise attack on Japan, in the event of a grave collision between the superpowers. As there were various problems to be solved between the two countries, such as the fishery issue, repatriation of Japanese detained in the USSR, and Soviet support for Japan's application to join the United Nations, the strategic advantage which the Soviet Union was deemed to enjoy under the extension of a state of war with Japan was seen as an effective bargaining counter against Japanese national interests.[5] Sugihara reached the conclusion that Japan should attempt to terminate the state of war through restoring diplomatic relations.

It should be emphasised that Hatoyama and Sugihara did not regard the Soviet Union as an immediate military threat to Japan. Rather, they appear to have been worried over the contingency of direct confrontation between the two superpowers. Their proposal for normalisation in 1952 reflected a sense of crisis based on their anxiety, whether reasonable or not, over an intensification in the cold war. Interestingly, at this stage neither Hatoyama nor Sugihara seemed to appreciate the softening in Soviet attitudes. Perhaps it was around 1954 when they were convinced of the certainty of the change in the Soviet position. Until then Hatoyama and Sugihara were dubious of the sincerity of the Soviet peace overtures.

In his book published in 1952, *Aru Daigishi No Seikatsu To Iken* (Views and Way of Life of a Dietman), Hatoyama expressed firm anti-Soviet views. He characterised the communist regime of the Soviet Union as 'anti-democratic' and went on to state that there was no freedom and no peace in such a regime.[6] Basically he considered the Soviet regime and communist regimes in general as 'dictatorship.'[7] He commented, 'We must not forget that a despotic state such as the Soviet Union necessarily adopts an aggressive foreign policy.'[8] The goal of Soviet foreign policy was defined by Hatoyama as 'unification of the world by Red Revolution.'[9] Gromyko's participation in the San Francisco peace conference and the Soviet proposal for an armistice in the Korean war were described by Hatoyama as examples of a Soviet 'peace offensive.' He pointed out that the real Soviet motivations were tactical and strategic, intended to divide the western allies and to reduce the speed of western rearmament.[10] He concluded: 'Metaphorically speaking, the peace offensive is like a hawk hiding its claws under its wings. The claws are hidden but still existing.'[11]

Hatoyama's advisers appear to have taken a similar view in 1952. Although Sugihara recognised slight favourable changes in the Soviet domestic situation and in the Soviet attitude towards Japan, he believed that the changes were not sufficient to demonstrate a fundamental alteration in the Soviet approach.

It is important to examine their views of the United States, although the evidence is limited. In his memoirs Hatoyama disclosed his suspicion of the Americans. Hatoyama held nationalistic ideas which included an element of anti-Americanism. In addition, he showed considerable doubt about the rationality and reliability of US conduct in international politics. These feelings may have arisen from his experience of being purged and even before that, of anger at the American use of the atomic bomb in August 1945; however, it seems clear that Hatoyama entertained more general doubts about the United States. He remarked that he had despised the Americans because he had encountered their irrationality and recklessness before the war.[12] More significantly he doubted American reliability in defending Japan in the event of war between the superpowers. In his book published in 1952 he repeated that the US-Japan security pact should be reinforced by Japanese troops. He cast doubt even on the credibility of the pact:

> ... Even with US-Japanese Security Pact, the US troops may retreat from Japan in the light of strategic necessity in case of overall devastation of international situations. If they do not retreat, they may reduce the forces. Then, Japan would face the necessity for rearmament.[13]

This statement was hypothetical but it cannot be denied that Hatoyama felt that Japan could not entirely depend on the credibility of US forces. This consideration led directly to recognition of the need to reduce the possibility of the outbreak of war between Japan and the USSR. It is likely that this factor compelled Hatoyama to launch the normalisation policy.

It could be argued that Hatoyama should have extended his policy into a more substantial improvement in Soviet-Japanese relations. But he could not do so. Firstly, because of the reservations he and his advisers felt about the Soviet Union. Moreover, in 1952 the cold war and East-West tension was at its height. Even mere normalisation must have seemed difficult to achieve. Secondly, the Hatoyama group knew very well that Japan could not survive without depending on US economic and military assistance.

In March 1953 Stalin died. This resulted in less harsh Soviet attitudes in international politics. The international situation seemed to change into an era of 'thaw.' At the beginning of 1954 the foreign ministers of the US, Britain, France and the USSR met in Berlin to discuss German problems. As regards to the Far East, the Korean war had ended with the armistice in July 1953: this was followed by the Geneva conference in 1954 whereby the five powers, namely the USA, the USSR, Britain, France and the People's Republic of China, managed to reach an agreement for a ceasefire in Indochina. As for the development of events relating more directly to Japan, the Soviet Union and China issued a joint declaration in October 1954, which contained a proposal for normalisation of relations with Japan and an agreement for the withdrawal of Soviet forces stationed at Port Arthur.

Despite these favourable omens for detente, the structure of confrontation between East and West still remained. Both superpowers were building up their nuclear stockpiles in the mid-1950s. Besides the arms race the mid-1950s saw intensification of tension through expansion of establishment of defence systems on both sides, particularly by the western allies. In Europe they included West Germany in the establishment of the West European Union in 1954, despite various Soviet attempts to prevent it. To counter a possible future threat from German rearmament, the Soviet Union set up the Warsaw Treaty Organisation in 1955. In the Far East various anti-communist defence arrangements were constructed: ANZUS in 1951, the US-Korean Mutual Security Pact, the US-Republic of China Mutual Defence Treaty in 1954. Japan had concluded a security pact with the United States in 1951; this was reinforced by the US-Japan Mutual Security Agreement in 1954.

Sugihara seems, at the latest in the spring of 1954, to have been aware of a substantial softening in Soviet policy towards Japan. In March and May 1954 the Polish overseas office in Paris approached its Japanese opposite number and proposed the restoration of diplomatic relations between Poland and Japan. According to Sugihara, the Polish proposal included a statement that, even without an alteration in US-Japanese relations, it would be possible to normalise relations between the two countries. He observed that this was a clear indication of significant change in Soviet policy towards Japan.[14] On 21 July 1954 Vyshinsky, the Soviet vice-foreign minister, told visiting members of the Japanese Diet that the Soviet Union hoped to restore diplomatic relations with Japan and to encourage cultural and economic exchanges; he added that his country was prepared to offer parole to Japanese war criminals. In September 1954 the Soviet foreign minister, Molotov, also revealed preparation for normalisation with Japan. The Sino-Soviet joint declaration in October 1954 called for the restoration of diplomatic relations with Japan. Sugihara was convinced of the certainty of the Soviet change by this development.

Matsumoto Shunichi, another of Hatoyama's advisers, discerned the significance of the evolving international situation. He recognised that Soviet policy had been based on the principle of peaceful co-existence since Stalin's death. He assumed that the Soviet Union was attempting to establish global detente and that Soviet proposals regarding Japan were designed to promote detente with the United States.[15] Hatoyama also became aware of the general changes in Soviet policy at the latest in the spring of 1955, although it is reasonable to assume that he had observed a change in international developments much earlier. In April 1955 the tone of his statements began to change. On 11 April he made clear before the Standing Committee for Foreign Affairs of the House of Councillors that he was convinced that the Soviet Union hoped to maintain peace in Asia and Europe.[16] In May he stated that the contingency of a third world war was receding.[17] In July he reiterated that the Soviet Union was now heading for world peace and that international tension had diminished.[18]

Although the trend of detente grew during the mid-1950s, Hatoyama and his advisers were still haunted with the danger of escalation in the cold war. Hatoyama remarked that normalisation should be achieved to prevent another 'hot war' from occurring around Japan.[19] This was inspired by the fear that Japan could be dragged into a future major war. They were not so naive as to believe that the trend of detente was irreversible and that it would overwhelm the cold war structure. But they do not seem to have feared an imminent threat from the Soviet Union. Rather, their anxiety was directed to the possibility of a third world war. In this sense, the United States, as well as the USSR, was perceived as a source of danger.

Hatoyama often quoted, however, his understanding of the general trend in detente to refute the anti-Soviet suspicion expressed by the anti-Hatoyama and anti-normalisation groups in Japan. His basic argument was that the Japanese did not have to be over-sensitive to Soviet intentions following normalisation: subversion through communist activities encouraged by the Soviet embassy. It is certain that the new world situation provided the Hatoyama group with a suitable opportunity to implement their normalisation policy. It created not only the feasibility of normalisation but assisted in neutralising the opposition from critics of normalisation in Japan.

Hatoyama also felt that Japan should participate in world politics and follow a rather more assertive line. Matsumoto recalled that the prime minister attempted to adapt Japanese policy to the main stream of peaceful co-existence.[20] The concept with regard to Japan's role may have created the pseudo-nationalistic character of their policy.[21] In his article in 1954 Hatoyama called for 'Heiwa Gaiko' (Peace Diplomacy) and suggested that Japan should contribute to the dissolution of the cold war by playing a role as a 'bridge' between both blocs.[22]

The pseudo-neutralist tendency was evidently based on the perceived relationship between ideology and diplomacy. For instance, Kono Ichiro, who was the most influential politician in the Hatoyama faction within the Democratic party and later within the Liberal-Democratic party, recalled that Hatoyama often suggested that Japan should have diplomatic relations with states whose ideological stance was different from Japan's.[23] Matsumoto and Sugihara agreed with Hatoyama. Matsumoto was convinced that ideology should be separated from diplomacy. He expressed admiration for Palmerston for this reason.[24] Sugihara recognised that the quintessence of international politics was not ideology but power struggles and that power struggles could sometimes be confused with ideological disputes.[25]

Hatoyama's policy was viewed by the American and British governments with suspicion: they feared that Japan might adopt a 'neutralist' position in the East-West confrontation. But the fact was that his foreign policy was remote from the so-called 'neutralist' policy advocated by non-aligned countries. Hatoyama understood that Japan could not survive without close ties with the USA. He once stated that it was not practical for Japan to take a neutralist policy because she had the US-Japan security pact.[26] When he referred to 'peace,' he meant what could be achieved by Japan's contribution to the western collective security system, specifically the security pact.[27] He made strenuous efforts to eradicate American suspicion that Japan would become a neutralist country. He frequently sent his close political adviser, Matsumoto (Frank) Takio, the vice general secretary of the Hatoyama cabinet, to the American embassy in Tokyo to explain that Hatoyama neither intended to move into the communist bloc nor to antagonise the US government. Matsumoto emphasised to American officials that Hatoyama was the most pro-American politician amongst those purged during the occupation.[28]

The Hatoyama group entertained the optimistic view that if Japan did not change her basic strategic or ideological stance, it might be feasible to secure a reduction in American pressure and control over Japanese foreign policy. Matsumoto Shunichi once wrote that he recognised that the United States was not almighty, implying that she could not always control the diplomatic conduct of her allies.[29] Matsumoto was influenced by his experience as ambassador in London between 1952 and 1954 during which period the British government sought a diminution in international tension. Although Anthony Eden and the Foreign Office were under great pressure from the United States to join an *ad hoc* defence arrangement termed a 'united front' by John Foster Dulles, Eden managed to achieve a ceasefire in the Indochina war by resisting American pressure. Apart from this, Churchill proposed a summit meeting including the Soviet Union in 1953. Matsumoto was encouraged in the belief that Japan could pursue a more independent policy.

In the mid-1950s US-Japanese relations encountered difficulty. Public opinion in Japan revealed anti-American sentiment, caused by the prolonged presence of American troops: this was intensified by the Fifth Lucky Dragon incident in the Bikini Atoll. In addition, nationalism developed considerably. At inter-governmental level problems resulted from US pressure on Japan to rearm and from the negotiations over the reduction in the Japanese financial burden for keeping American bases in Japan. Shigemitsu Mamoru, the then foreign minister, is reported as saying that existing relations resembled those between the two powers shortly before the start of the Pacific war. In these circumstances the Hatoyama government faced a dilemma. They required support from those urging a more nationalistic approach. Hatoyama was very anxious over the serious repercussions of vocal anti-American sentiment. In 1951, although he had not yet been depurged, he met Dulles and handed him a letter. His concern at hostility to America was apparent.[30] After he became prime minister he sent Dulles a letter, promising to sweep away anti-American feeling in Japan.[31] The normalisation policy has to be seen as part of the solution to this dilemma. Sugihara Arata wrote as follows in a short article discussing policy towards the Soviet Union:

> The basic principle is the same. What is different is whether we should follow it too strictly or rather loosely. Opposing the latter, some argue that we have to observe the principle very strictly because it demonstrates our loyalty. But some others argue that from the broader and long-term point of view it is better to follow the principle loosely and that it would make the principle itself sounder.[32]

In this passage, 'the basic principle' means that Japan should adopt a pro-American stance and be a member of the free world. Sugihara believed that slightly looser relations with the United States would strengthen the relationship. To Sugihara, too dependent and passive an attitude towards the USA seemed unsound. He suggested that nationalism should not be suppressed and that the US should pay respect to the nationalism of her allies.[33] It is reasonable to deduce that Sugihara tried to find some outlet for nationalistic sentiment and to calm down anti-Americanism.

III NATIONALISM OF HATOYAMA: RESTORATION OF JAPAN'S INTERNATIONAL STATUS AND ANTI-AMERICANISM

Following Japan's surrender in 1945, national reconstruction had been the main objective of Japanese political leaders who, after the occupation, faced the necessity of shaping the future development of their country. Yoshida Shigeru intended to achieve this objective by strengthening close ties with the United States. The peace treaty with the free nations symbolised independence for him. He tried to raise Japan's international status through making his country an important ally for the US in the Far East in the context of the cold war. Undoubtedly, these reconstruction policies advocated by Yoshida reflected his own nationalistic sentiments. Hatoyama's foreign policy was also based on his nationalism, though its form of embodiment was different.

Hatoyama's nationalism had at least the following two fundamental characteristics. Firstly, he tended to attach positive value to the pre-war Japan of the pre-militarisation period. Secondly, his nationalism had an anti-American dimension. His attitude towards the Soviet-Japanese normalisation was influenced by these two factors. Hatoyama considered that Japan's entry into the Second World War was an aberration in her history caused by the militarist and defeatist Dietmen.[34] He tended to argue that Japan should go back to the normal course of Japanese history existing before the Showa militarisation period. There is no doubt that he strongly desired Japan to revert to her international status enjoyed during the 'normal' period. His general approach to the formulation of foreign policy reflected his desire for the promotion of Japan's international status. 'Peace Diplomacy' proposed by Hatoyama connoted preventing an escalation in the cold war: Japan must act as a bridge between East and West .[35] He wished to raise Japan's status by assigning her to a role of a contributor to reduction of East-West tensions. Moreover, it cannot be denied that he aimed at obtaining a stronger position towards the US by exerting an influence on Soviet-US relations. Here it has to be noted that he attempted to combine the nationalistic goal of Japan with her international goal.[36] Hatoyama tried to direct nationalism, both his own and that of the Japanese public, towards the objective of reducing international tensions. It is hardly necessary to say that the normalisation policy was regarded as the main instrument of 'Peace Diplomacy.' One of his specific policy goals was to obtain membership of the UN. This would enhance Japan's status. But Japanese applications faced a continuous Soviet veto. It was appreciated in Tokyo that the absence of normal diplomatic relations with the USSR inhibited Japan's entry into the UN. It was an urgent task to restore relations.

It has to be understood that Hatoyama personally was critical of the United States. It has often been stated that Hatoyama and others surrounding him, such as Kono Ichiro, Miki Bukichi and Ishibashi Tanzan, became anti-American after they were purged.[37] As far as Hatoyama was concerned, however, his critical views were rooted earlier. He expressed hostile feelings shortly after the Pacific war ended. In September 1945 Hatoyama wrote an article in *Asahi Shimbun* entitled 'A Design for a New Party.' He stated that:

> What should we do to reconstruct Japan after the war? So long as the Americans insisted that 'Justice is power,' they cannot deny that the use of the A-bomb and indiscriminate murder of civilians are war crimes and the cases of violation of international law which are worse than attacks on hospital ships or the use of poison gas. We have to make them appreciate the disastrous situation of the afflicted areas and let them feel the necessity to compensate for what they have done and the responsibility for the reconstruction of those areas.[38]

In addition, he criticised the dissolution of the *zaibatsu* which he deemed reckless.[39] These doubts about the Americans led Hatoyama to adopt a foreign policy designed to reduce the likelihood of a war between the superpowers. Also, his anti-Americanism drove him to construct a policy whereby Japan could enjoy more freedom of activitity from the US. Normalising Soviet-Japanese relations was a suitable policy for this purpose.

IV CONCLUSION

The following conclusions can be arrived at. The Hatoyama group's proposal for the normalisation policy reflected their perception of international situations. The fear for the possibility of a third world war and of Japan being dragged into it led them to feel the need to improve Russo-Japanese relations or at least to reduce the contingency of an undeclared attack on Japan from the Soviet Union. At the same time, they assumed that the new trend of detente had emerged with great significance in international politics. They intended to join this new stream of international development and regarded world trends as encouraging for normalisation. However, this policy had to be pursued within certain limitations imposed by Japanese dependence on American military and economic assistance. Perceiving the continuance of a fundamental cold war structure, they had to carry out their detente policy without damaging relations with the United States. In this sense, the normalisation policy was a restricted detente policy.

Apart from their perception of international situations, Hatoyama's nationalistic desire for higher international status of Japan and for more freedom of activity from American pressures drove him to adopt the normalisation policy. At the period of reconstruction, and adhering to his memory of the past 'glory' of Japan, Hatoyama's normalisation policy could not escape from the influence of his nationalism.

Thus, Hatoyama's normalisation policy was a product of the fusion between the Hatoyama group's perception of the new international situation and Hatoyama's nationalism which contained a rather nostalgic tendency.

NOTES

1. Hatoyama Ichiro, *Htoyama Ichiro Kaikoroku* (Memoirs of Hatoyama Ichiro), Tokyo, 1957, p. 11. (Hereafter cited as *Kaikoroku*).
2. Sugihara Arata, *Gaikō no Kangaekata* (How To Understand Diplomacy), Tokyo, 1965, Chap. 8.
3. Sugihara, *ibid*, p. 89.
4. *Ibid.*, p. 113.
5. *Ibid.*
6. Hatoyama Ichiro, Aru *Daigishi no Seikatsu to Iken* (Views and Way of Life of a Dietman), Tokyo, 1952, p. 252, p. 262.
7. *Ibid.*, p. 263.
8. *Ibid.*, p. 262.
9. *Ibid.*, p. 262.
10. *Ibid.*, pp. 268-9.
11. *Ibid.*, p. 271.

12. Hatoyama, *Hatoyama Ichiro Kaikoroku*, p. 51.

13. Hatoyama, Aru *Daigishi no Seikatsu to Iken*, p. 288.

14. Sugihara, *op. cit.*, Chap. 8.

15. Matsumoto Shunichi, 'Hoppo Ryodo Mondai' (The Northern Territories Problems) *Kyōsanken Mondai* (Problems in the Communist Bloc), Vol. 13, No. 12, Tokyo, 1969, p. 8.

16. Asahi Shinbun, 11 April 1955.

17. Asahi, 15 May 1955.

18. Asahi, 14 July 1955.

19. Hatoyama Ichiro, 'Yoshida-kun No Yarikata Wa Machigatte Iru' (The Course of Yoshida is Wrong), *Chuōkōron*, Tokyo, November 1954, p. 173.

20. Matsumoto Shunichi, 'Soren Ni Tsukai Shite' (As I Saw in the Soviet Union as the Plenipotentiary) *Sekai Shūhō*, Vol. 38, No. 1, Tokyo, 1957, p. 66.

21. The idea of standing in between the two blocs has basic similarity to the so-called neutralist foreign policy. But the key of Hatoyama's foreign policy was to maintain cooperative relations with the US and to base the defence of Japan on the American military forces and alliance with her. In this sense, Hatoyama's foreign policy, especially his Soviet policy, cannot be characterised as 'neutralist' foreign policy, which was taken by the India of Nehru or by the Leftist Socialist party of Japan. That is the reason why I described it as 'pseudo-neutralistic' policy.

22. Hatoyama, *op. cit.*, p. 173.

23. Kono Ichiro, *Imadakara Hanaso* (Now I Will Talk About All), Tokyo, 1958, p. 8.

24. Matsumoto Shunichi, 'Gaiko to Kokkai,' (Diplomacy and the National Diet), *Chuōkōron*, Tokyo, July 1956, p. 56.

25. Sugihara, *op. cit.*, p. 3. Sugihara, 'Taiso Gaikō No Kokoro Gamae' (How To Cope With The Soviet Union) *Chuōkōron*, Tokyo, April 1955, p. 146, p. 151.

26. Asahi, 27 May 1955.

27. Hatoyama, *Kaikoroku*, p. 117.

28. Memorandum of conversation between Takizō Matsumoto and J. Craham Parsons, 6 April 1955. Records of the Office of Northeast Asian Affairs, Lot 58 D118, T.3.1, National Archives of the United States, Washington D.C.

29. Matsumoto Shunichi, 'Nisso Kōshō Wa Dōnaruka' (How Will the Soviet-Japanese Negotiations Develop?) *Jitsugyō No Nihon*, Vol. 59, No. 15, Tokyo, 1956, p. 58.

30. Hatoyama, *Kaikoroku*, p. 87.

31. Asahi, 13 January 1955.

32. Sugihara, 'Taiso Gaikō No Kokorogamae,' p. 147.

33. Sugihara, *Gaikō No Kangaekata*, p. 70.

34. A manuscript for party broadcasting prepared by Hatoyama for election campaign on 13 October 1945. Quoted by Itoh Takashi, in '"Jiyushugisha" Hatoyama Ichiro - Sono Senzen, Senchu, Sengo -' (Liberalist Hatoyama Ichiro: Pre-War, Wartime and Post-War) *Taiheiyō Sensō, Journal of Modern Japanese Studies*, No. 4 (Tokyo, 1982), p. 77.

35. Hatoyama, 'Yoshidakun No Yarikata...' p. 173, Hatoyama, *Kaikoroku*, p. 198.

36. Sugihara, *op. cit.*, pp. 67-70.

37. Kosaka Masataka, *Saishō Yoshida Shigeru* (Tokyo, 1968), p. 91.

38. Hatoyama, *Kaikoroku*, p. 50.

39. *Ibid.*

Index